Presents from the Kitchen

Preserves • Pickles •
Marinades

NAUMANN & GÖBEL

Presents from the Kitchen

Preserves • Pickles • Marinades

© Naumann & Göbel Verlagsgesellschaft mbH, a subsidiary of
VEMAG Verlags- und Medien Aktiengesellschaft, Cologne
www.apollo-intermedia.de

Complete production: Naumann & Göbel Verlagsgesellschaft mbH, Cologne
Printed in Germany

ISBN 3–625–11179–9

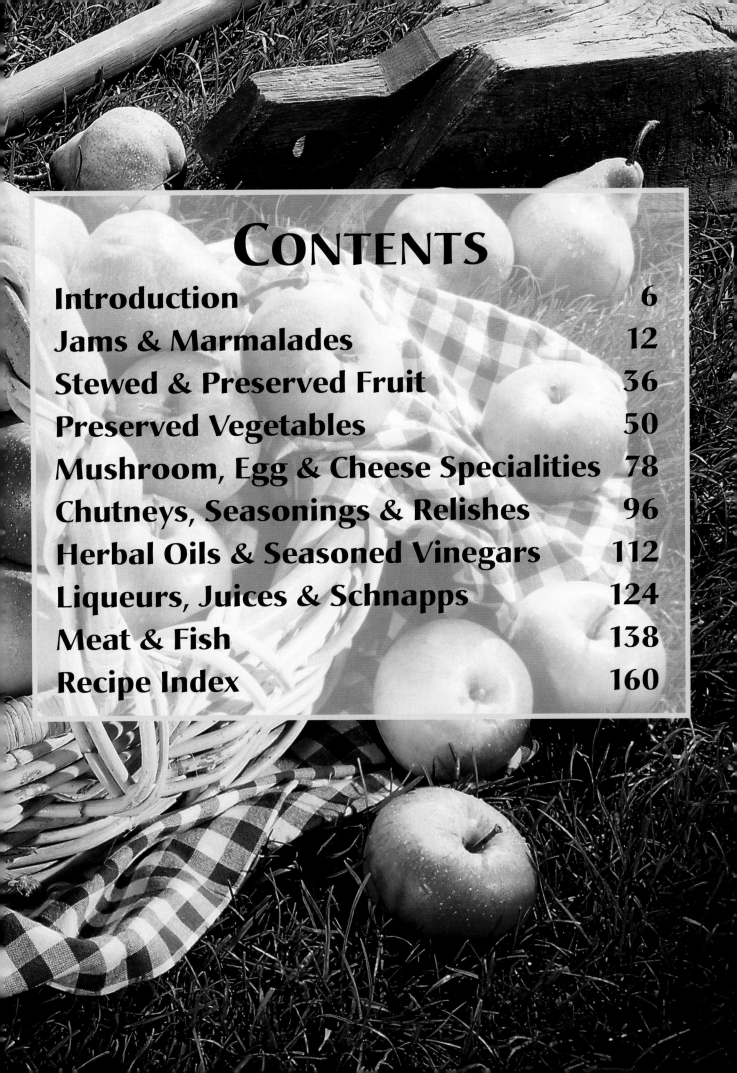

CONTENTS

INTRODUCTION

Preparing jams, marmalades and jellies is an art with a long tradition, is easy to learn, and the pleasure to be gained from enjoying aromatic homemade products throughout the year is one that binds people together. Let your fantasy and your taste preferences guide you to create fruity pleasures and pickled vegetable specialities that bring a summer breeze to your kitchen even on a cold winter's day. You will be amazed just how quickly you achieve good results, as long as you observe a few rules.

No special equipment is required for preserving. Most of the recipes require only everyday kitchen utensils. It is best to have everything at hand before you start: you will need a sharp kitchen knife, a fruit pitter, a mixing spoon, a skimmer, a ladle, a funnel, oven gloves, bowls, a colander, a hand blender, a chopping board and clean dishcloths.

Preserving Tips and Tricks
A crucial factor for successfully making jam, marmalade or jelly is the **quality** of fruit or vegetables used. Only fresh, fully

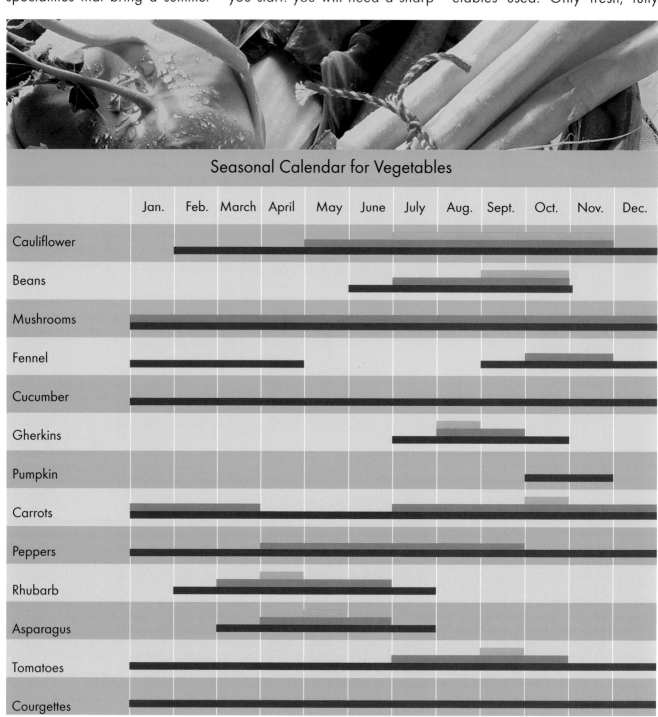

Seasonal Calendar for Vegetables

	Jan.	Feb.	March	April	May	June	July	Aug.	Sept.	Oct.	Nov.	Dec.
Cauliflower												
Beans												
Mushrooms												
Fennel												
Cucumber												
Gherkins												
Pumpkin												
Carrots												
Peppers												
Rhubarb												
Asparagus												
Tomatoes												
Courgettes												

ripe produce should be used. Over ripe, slightly off, or not sufficiently ripened produce is not suitable.

Wash the **fruit and vegetables** just before chopping to prevent their aroma from leaching. Delicate fruit such as handpicked raspberries or blackberries are an exception. They lose too much juice, and therefore aroma, when washed. They should be gently cleaned with a cloth or small brush. Soft fruits should always be used as quickly as possible after purchase or harvesting, as their aroma is reduced by storage.

The jars used for preserving must be immaculate. Jars with **twist-off lids** are recommended, as they are airtight, practical and hygienic. They protect the contents both from drying out and from microorganisms. If the contents are to be sterilised, then preserving jars with lids and rubber seals should be used.

The **rubber seals** should be boiled and then left to stand in the hot water until they are used.

A pan with a wide diameter is most suitable for the process of preserving. It should, however, only be filled to the half way point with fruit and sugar to prevent the mixture from boiling over during cooking.

Thoroughly wash the jars, preferably in a dishwasher, and rinse them several times in clear water. Boil the lids in a mixture of vinegar and water, rinse them in hot water and drain well.

Preserving sugar and jam sugar are always good choices when preserving. In both cases, the instructions on the packets should be followed exactly.

The classical method is to cook fruit and preserving sugar **in a ratio of 1 to 1**, that is, 1 lb of sugar for every 1 lb of fruit (or 1 kg of sugar for every 1 kg of fruit). This method results in a jam or jelly with a lovely aroma and an appetising colour that will also keep for a long time.

Even fruitier results are achieved when the fruit is mixed with jam sugar **in a ration of 2 to 1**. For every 1 lb of fruit, $^1/_2$ lb of jam sugar is added (or 1 kg of fruit for every 500 g of jam sugar). Jam sugar contains pectin and additional preservatives (citric and possibly ascorbic acid) because the natural preserving properties of sugar cannot fully develop at this ratio of fruit to sugar.

Skimming is necessary to clarify jellies or jams with fruit that contains a high level of protein, such as strawberries. Skimming should always be done after the cooking process has been completed.

To **test the set**, spoon 1 or 2 teaspoons of the hot mixture onto a cold surface or a saucer. The jam should set immediately. If it does not set, cook it slightly longer, or add citric acid. Citric acid lends firmness without impairing taste.

When it is ready, the jars are filled to the brim with the hot mixture. Tightly seal the jars immediately and **stand them upside down** for 5 to 10 minutes to allow air bubbles to surface. The vacuum thus created sterilises the hollow of the lid.

Alcohol preserves and enhances flavour. However, high percentage alcohol should always be added at the end of cooking. Replace the alcohol with fruit juice or just leave it out altogether if the preserve is to be eaten by children.

Ingredients such as **sultanas, walnuts, herbs or pine nuts** are better distributed in the mixture when the freshly filled and sealed jars are repeatedly turned while cooling.

Labels that detail in writing the contents and date of production are practical and a visually appealing way of identifying the mixture in the jars.

Fruit Preserving Calendar

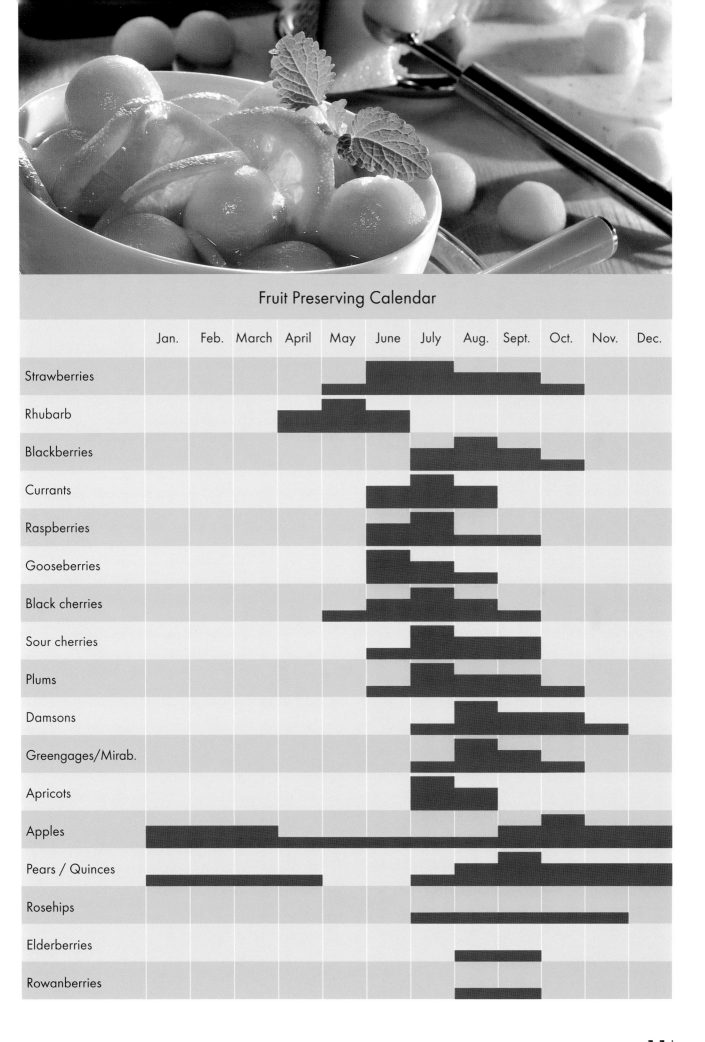

	Jan.	Feb.	March	April	May	June	July	Aug.	Sept.	Oct.	Nov.	Dec.
Strawberries					■	■	■	■	■	■		
Rhubarb				■	■	■						
Blackberries							■	■	■	■		
Currants						■	■	■				
Raspberries						■	■	■	■			
Gooseberries						■	■					
Black cherries					■	■	■	■				
Sour cherries						■	■	■				
Plums						■	■	■	■	■		
Damsons							■	■	■	■		
Greengages/Mirab.							■	■	■			
Apricots						■	■					
Apples	■	■	■	■	■			■	■	■	■	■
Pears / Quinces	■	■	■	■			■	■	■	■	■	■
Rosehips							■	■	■	■		
Elderberries								■	■			
Rowanberries								■				

JAMS & MARMALADES

APPLE JELLY WITH HERBS

Tip

For an especially rich green colour, you can add 2–3 drops of green food colouring to this jelly.

Makes 4 450 ml/16 fl oz

1.5 kg/3 lb 5 oz apples
   (e.g. Cox Orange, Ingrid Marie)
500 ml/18 fl oz water
150 g/5 oz sugar
1 stick of cinnamon
4–6 cloves
1 kg/2¼ lb preserving sugar
1 lemon
Fresh herbs, washed and dried
   (e.g. mint, thyme, sage)

1 Wash the apples, rub them dry and remove the cores. Chop the fruit into small pieces. Add the apple pieces to the water, sugar (not the preserving sugar) and spices, and boil for 20–25 minutes until soft.

2 Drain the resulting juice through a cloth. Set the apple pulp to the side; it can later be used for making compote.

3 Measure out 1½ pints/1 litre of the apple juice, topping up with water or fruit juice if necessary. Slowly bring the juice to the boil while stirring and gradually pouring in the preserving sugar. Allow the jelly to boil fiercely for about 15 minutes until the set test succeeds.

4 Add the herbs of your choice to the jelly mixture and gently stir them in. Pour the mixture into the jars and seal tightly. Leave to stand until the jelly has set.

HOT TOMATO PRESERVE

Makes 2 230 ml/8 fl oz jars

500 g/1 lb 2 oz tomatoes
500 g/1 lb 2 oz jam sugar (1 to 1)
1 small hot chilli
1 clove

1 Scald the tomatoes in boiling water then plunge into cold water and remove skins. Halve them, remove the seeds and dice. Clean the chilli, remove the seeds and finely chop.

2 Mix together the chilli, tomatoes and jam sugar. Leave to stand overnight in a cool place.

3 The next day, place the chilli-tomato-sugar mixture into a large pan together with the clove, bring to the boil, and boil fiercely for 4 minutes while stirring.

4 Remove the clove and straight-away pour the mixture into twist-off jars, which have been rinsed in hot water. Seal the jars tightly, and turn the jars upside down for 5 minutes.

Tip
Hot tomato preserve tastes delicious with grilled meat, or simply on its own on a piece of crusty baguette.

15

TART LIME MARMALADE

Tip
Instead of limes, oranges flavoured with Grand Marnier can be used in this recipe.

Makes 6 450 ml/16 fl oz jars

750 g/1 lb 11 oz limes
1.5 l/2 pints 13 fl oz water
300 ml/10 ½ fl oz green orange liqueur
2 kg/4 lb 7 oz sugar
225 g/8 oz (½ bottle) liquid pectin

1 Rinse the limes, rub them dry and cut into thin slices. Cover with water and leave to soak overnight.

2 Place the limes in a pan, reserving the water in which they had soaked, and simmer for 1 hour over a low heat.

3 Remove the fruit with a skimmer, weigh it, and bring up to 1.2 kg/ 2 lb 10 oz by adding the water from soaking. Stir in the sugar and liqueur and bring to the boil while stirring. Boil fiercely for 2 minutes.

4 Stir in the liquid gelling agent and bring the mixture briefly to the boil. Stir in the additional citric acid (if included with the pectin).

5 Pour the marmalade into rinsed twist-off jars straightaway, close the lids and stand the jars upside down for 5 minutes.

Orange Marmalade

Makes 3–4 450 ml/16 fl oz jars

500 g/1 lb 2 oz untreated oranges
1 kg/2¼ lb jam sugar
125 ml/4 ½ fl oz water

1 Thoroughly rinse the oranges in hot water and carefully rub dry. Allow to cool. Either grate the rind finely or peel extremely thinly and cut into very fine strips. Remove the pith. Cut the flesh into small pieces.

2 Combine the flesh of the fruit, the grated peel, the jam sugar and the water in a pan. Bring to the boil and cook the mixture fiercely for a further 4 minutes.

3 Fill the rinsed twist-off jars with the marmalade, close the lids, turn the jars upside down and leave them to stand for 5 minutes.

Tip
This marmalade can also be made using Seville oranges.

GARDEN FRUIT PRESERVES

STRAWBERRY JAM WITH A SHOT

Makes about 9
225 ml/8 fl oz jars

1 kg/2¹/₄ lb strawberries
1 kg/2¹/₄ lb jam sugar
1–2 lemons
40 ml/2 Tbsp orange liqueur

1 Wash the strawberries, remove the stalks, drain and then cut the fruit into pieces.

2 Rinse the lemons in hot water and grate their rinds.

3 Mix together the strawberries, the preserving sugar and 2 Tbsp of the lemon rind. In a large pan, bring the mixture to a rolling boil for 4 minutes, stirring all the time. Stir in the orange liqueur and then pour the mixture into clean jars. Tightly close the lids straightaway.

RASPBERRY JAM WITH A SHOT

Makes about 6
225 ml/8 fl oz jars

1 kg/2¹/₄ lb raspberries
1 kg/2¹/₄ lb jam sugar
125 ml/4¹/₂ fl oz himbeergeist
(raspberry schnapps)

1 Sort the raspberries by hand. Combine them with the jam sugar, cover and allow to stand for 24 hours.

2 In a large pan, bring the fruit-sugar mixture to a rolling boil for 4 minutes.

3 Remove from the heat, stir in the raspberry schnapps thoroughly, then fill clean jars with the mixture. Tightly close the jars.

ROSE PRESERVE

Makes 3 3¹/₂ fl oz/100 ml jars

250 g/9 oz red rose petals
1 kg/2¹/₄ lb icing sugar

1 Sort the rose petals, selecting only undamaged ones; wash them and dab them dry.

2 Mix the petals with the icing sugar on a baking sheet. Using a rolling pin, roll over the petals until they become a thick mass.

3 Rinse the jars with boiling water, fill them with the rose petal mixture and immediately close airtight.

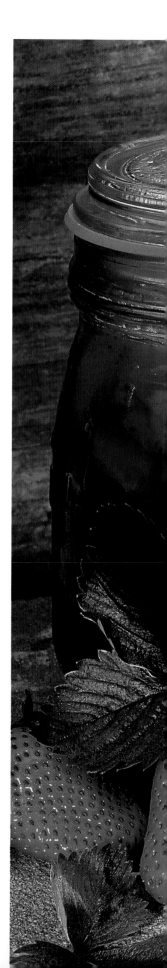

ROSE PETAL JELLY

Makes 3 200 ml/7 fl oz jars

500 g/1 lb 2 oz dark red rose petals
Juice of 2 untreated lemons
500 ml/18 fl oz orange juice
200 g/7 oz castor sugar
800 g/1¾ lb jam sugar

1 Allow the rose petals to soak overnight in 250 ml/9 fl oz water combined with the lemon juice.

2 Remove the petals with a skimmer, and place the remaining liquid in a pan with the orange juice.

3 First stir in the castor sugar, then the jam sugar, and bring the mixture to the boil for approximately 1 minute.

4 Add the rose petals and boil for another 3 minutes. Finally, fill the jars to the brim and seal well.

MELON JELLY

Makes 4 250 ml/9 fl oz jars

1 untreated orange
1/2 **watermelon (approx. 500 g/1 lb 2 oz)**
3 Tbsp Campari
8 Tbsp orange juice
1 packet 2:1 pectin

1 Thoroughly wash the oranges in hot water and cut into slices. Cut out the flesh of the melon and remove the seeds. Chop the fruit into small pieces, place in a sieve and press out the juice. This should yield about 400 ml/14 fl oz of liquid.

2 Mix the Campari and orange juice with the melon juice and top up with water to reach 750 ml/1 pint 7 fl oz. Add the pectin to the mixture in a pan and bring to the boil over a high heat, stirring all the time.

3 Halve the orange slices and arrange them in the jars. Bring the juice mixture to a rolling boil for 2 to 3 minutes, then fill the prepared jars.

4 Seal the jars well and stand them upside down. Turn the jars around before the jelly has set completely.

Information

Watermelons can weigh up to 5 kg/ 11 lb. A full 95% of its flesh is made up of water, and in times of drought people have even used them as a source of water.

PUMPKIN PRESERVE

Makes 8 250 ml/9 fl oz jars

1 kg/2¼ lb pumpkin flesh
¾ tsp ground cinnamon
½ tsp finely chopped ginger
¼ tsp powdered cloves
1 large pinch grated nutmeg
6 Tbsp lemon juice
1 kg/2¼ lb jam sugar

1 Cut the pumpkin flesh into cubes and pass through a mincer using the finest disk.

2 Stew the minced pumpkin in a pan with a small amount of water for about 10 minutes. Then stir in the cinnamon, ginger, powdered cloves, nutmeg and lemon juice.

3 Sprinkle in the jam sugar and bring everything to the boil, stirring continuously. After boiling for 5 minutes, fill the jars and seal straightaway. This preserve goes well with game dishes.

APPLE JELLY WITH CALVADOS

Makes 5 250 ml/9 fl oz jars

1 kg/2¼ lb apples (e.g. Boskop)
4 cloves
5 cinnamon sticks
¼ tsp grated lemon peel
3 Tbsp lemon juice
500 g/1 lb 2 oz jam sugar 2:1
2 Tbsp vanilla essence
20 ml/1 Tbsp Calvados
5 star aniseeds

1 The day before making the jelly, heat the oven to 260 °C/500 °F/ gas mark 9. Wash the apples, roughly chop them, and add to an ovenproof pot together with the cloves, 2 of the cinnamon sticks and the lemon peel. Pour in 500 ml/18 fl oz of water and bring the apples to the boil in the covered pot in the oven. Simmer for approximately 15 minutes then leave to stand in the pot overnight.

2 Pass the apple mixture and its juice through a sieve lined with a cloth. Allow the juice to pass through, pressing the apples well.

3 Mix the resulting juice with the lemon juice. Measure out about 750 ml/1¼ pints of liquid, add the jam sugar and vanilla essence, and bring to a rolling boil for 3 minutes while stirring. Blend in the Calvados. Place a little of the mixture onto a small plate to test for set.

4 Briefly scald the star aniseeds in boiling water. Halve the remaining cinnamon sticks. Stand the prepared jars on a damp cloth, add a star aniseed and a half a cinnamon stick to each jar, fill to the brim with the hot jelly and seal the lids.

Tip
This jelly can also be made with apple juice bought from a shop. Just boil it up with the spices, then allow it to draw and cool before proceeding.

WILD FRUIT AND GARDEN FRUIT PRESERVES

ROSEHIP PRESERVE WITH RED WINE

Makes 7 250 ml/9 fl oz jars

750 g/1 lb 11 oz rosehips
    (weight after removal of seeds)
0.7 l/1¼ pints red wine
750 g/1 lb 11 oz honey

1 Remove the stalks from the rose-hips, cut them open and carefully scrape out the furry seeds. Wash the deseeded rosehips thoroughly and dab dry with kitchen paper. Place them in a large glass and pour the wine over top.

2 Leave to stand in a cool place for 24 hours. Strain off and retain the wine. Stirring constantly, boil the wine with the honey into a thick syrup.

3 Pass the rosehips through a sieve. Stir the pulp into the syrup and return to the boil. Fill the jars with the hot mixture and seal immediately.

DAMSON JAM

Makes 5 500 ml/18 fl oz jars

3 kg/6 lb 10 oz late damsons
3 cinnamon sticks
40 ml/2 Tbsp damson schnapps
(Slivovitz)

1 Halve the damsons and remove the stones. Place the fruit on a deep baking tray and bake at 200 °C/390 °F/gas mark 6 for 1 hour, then thicken at 160 °C/320 °F/gas mark 2–3 for a further hour. Remove from the oven and turn into a pan.

2 Puree the damson to a pulp, add the cinnamon sticks and simmer over a low heat for 2 hours, stirring occasionally.

3 Stir in the schnapps, remove the cin-namon sticks, fill the jars and seal.

ELDERBERRY AND PLUM JAM

Makes 4 250 ml/9 fl oz jars

250 g/9 oz plums
750 g/1 lb 11 oz elderberries
    (without stalks)
500 g/1 lb 2 oz icing sugar

1 Wash and halve the plums, re-move the stones and cut into quar-ters. Wash and dry the elderberries and combine with the plums in a large bowl. Sprinkle with the icing sugar and leave in a cool place overnight.

2 The next day, bring the fruit mixture to the boil and cook for about 25 minutes over a medium heat until it has thickened. Fill clean jars with the boiling hot mixture and seal immediately.

APPLE AND CARROT JELLY

Tip

This recipe uses special diet fructose. The jelly is therefore suitable for diabetics and calorie watchers.

Makes 4-5 16 fl oz/450ml jars

10–15 small lemon balm leaves
2 pints/1.2 l apple juice
200 g/7 oz grated carrot
500 g/1 lb 2 oz diet fructose

1 Wash the lemon balm, shake dry and cut into thin strips.

2 Mix well the apple juice, grated carrot and fructose in a pan.

Stirring continuously, bring to a rolling boil over a high heat for 4 minutes.

3 Stir in the lemon balm as soon as the jelly begins to set.

4 Fill well rinsed jars with the jelly, seal the lids and stand upside down for approximately 5 minutes.

TOMATO AND LEMON JAM

Makes 6–7 230 ml/8 fl oz jars

1 kg/2¼ lb red tomatoes
Juice and grated peel of
        2 untreated lemons
1 kg/2¼ lb jam sugar 1:1

1 Wash the tomatoes, remove the green stalk eyes and puree the fruit with a hand blender.

2 Thoroughly mix the tomato puree, lemon juice and peel, and jam sugar together in a large pan, cover, and leave to stand for 2 to 3 hours. Then, stirring, bring to a rolling boil for 4 minutes.

3 Immediately fill twist-off jars rinsed in hot water with the tomato mixture, seal tight and stand upside down for 5 minutes.

Tip
Unusual but with a convincingly fruity freshness: this preserve with just a hint of the Mediterranean turns bread and jam into a tasty experience.

PRESERVES FOR THE CALORIE WATCHER

PINEAPPLE AND GINGER PRESERVE

Makes 2 250 ml/9 fl oz jars

1 pineapple (about 500 g/1 lb 2 oz fruit)
1 small piece ginger (15 g/¹/₂ oz)
Juice and peel of 1 untreated lime
1 packet pectin (10 g/¹/₃ oz)
3 tsp liquid sweetener
5 sheets of clear gelatine
1 large pinch citric acid

1 Cut the pineapple into rings. Peel the rings and remove the wooden core. Cut half the rings into cubes, and puree the other half in a blender. Peel and grate the ginger.

2 Stir together the fruit, the pectin, the lime juice and peel, and the ginger. Sweeten with the liquid sweetener. Soften the gelatine in a little water.

3 Allow to stand for 20–30 minutes, then slowly bring to a rolling boil while stirring. Boil for 1¹/₂ minutes, then stir in the wrung-out gelatine.

4 Fill the prepared jars with the hot fruit mixture. Sprinkle citric acid over the top of the preserve and seal the jar lids tightly.

KIWI AND GRAPEFRUIT PRESERVE

Makes 2 250 ml/9 fl oz jars

4 kiwis (approx. 420 g/1 lb)
1 grapefruit (300 g/10¹/₂ oz)
1 packet pectin (10 g/¹/₃ oz)
3 Tbsp liquid sweetener
4 sheets clear gelatine
1 large pinch citric acid

1 Thinly peel the kiwis and trim the ends. Cut 2 kiwis into slices, and crush the rest.

2 Peel the grapefruit, remove the white pith, and cut out the fruit filets from the segments with a sharp knife, retaining the juice.

3 Mix all the fruit together with the pectin in a pot and leave to stand for 30 minutes. Soften the gelatine in a little water. Then slowly heat the fruit while stirring constantly. Add the liquid sweetener and bring to a rolling boil for 1 minute. Stir in the wrung-out gelatine.

4 Fill the prepared jars with the hot mixture. Sprinkle the citric acid over the top and seal the lids tightly.

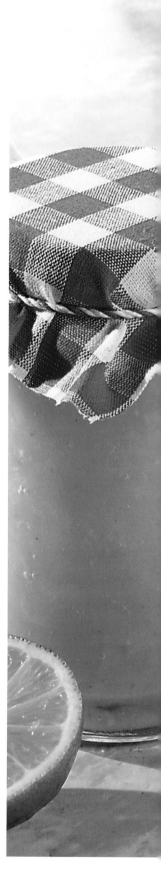

Tip
When making jam
with sweeteners,
gelatine or special
low-sugar or no-
sugar pectin must be
used to achieve a
good consistency,
since sugar itself
is the principle
gelling agent in
traditional jams.

FRUIT JUICE PRESERVES

GRAPE JUICE AND KIWI PRESERVE

Makes 2 230 ml/8 fl oz jars

300 ml/10½ fl oz white grape juice
300 g/10½ oz kiwis
1 Tbsp set honey
170 g/5¾ oz jam sugar
Juice of ½ lemon
½ tsp cinnamon

1 Mix the grape juice with the jam sugar and, stirring continuously, bring to a rolling boil for at least a minute. Let the grape jelly cool slightly.

2 Peel the kiwis, cut into slices and puree. Stir together the kiwi puree, the honey, the lemon juice and the cinnamon.

3 Add the cooled grape jelly to the kiwi puree and stir well. Finally, fill prepared jars with the mixture and seal. The fresh jam will keep for 10 to 14 days in the refrigerator.

GRAPE JUICE–PUNCH JELLY

Makes 2–3 450 ml/16 fl oz jars

1 l/1¾ pints red grape juice
5 cloves
3–4 cinnamon sticks
Grated peel of ½ lemon
Grated peel of ½ orange
560 g/1 lb 4 oz jam sugar

1 Mix together the grape juice, the spices and the orange and lemon peel, and bring to the boil. Boil the fruit punch for 10 to 15 minutes, then set aside to cool.

2 Remove the cloves and the cinnamon from the punch, stir in the jam sugar and mix well. Bring to a rolling boil for at least 1 minute.

3 Fill clean, rinsed twist-off jars with the grape juice punch and store well sealed in the refrigerator.

CHERRY AND WALNUT PRESERVE

Makes approximately 6 230 ml/8 fl oz jars

1 untreated orange
100 g/3½ oz walnut kernels
1 kg/2¼ lb sour cherries
200 ml/7 fl oz elderberry juice
500 g/1 lb 2 oz jam sugar 2:1
2–3 sprigs unsprayed lavender
        (alternatively 2–3 tsp dried
        lavender)

1 Wash the orange in hot water, finely grate the rind, then press the juice out of the orange.

2 Roast the walnut kernels in a non-stick pan without oil until they begin to release their aroma, then leave to cool. Wash and stone the sour cherries.

3 Weigh out 850 g/1 lb 14 oz of the cherries, put them in a large pan and puree with a hand blender. Stir in the orange juice, peel, nuts, elderberry juice and jam sugar. Pluck the lavender blossoms from the stalks, add to the mixture and bring to the boil.

4 Boil everything for 4 minutes, stirring continuously, then immediately pour the mixture into twist-off jars rinsed with hot water, filling them to the brim. Seal the jars well, then turn upside down for 5 minutes.

Tip
Careful cleaning of the glass rim of each jar is recommended to ensure the jars seal well and can easily be opened.

SUMMER FRUIT PLEASURES

RHUBARB JELLY

Makes 4 500 ml/18 fl oz jars

2 kg/4 lb 7 oz rhubarb
1 kg/2¼ lb green apples
Juice of 2 lemons
Jam sugar according
           to amount of juice

1 Wash the rhubarb and the apples. Cut the unpeeled apples into eighths and remove the cores. Cut the rhubarb up into pieces.

2 Put the apples and rhubarb into a large pan. Add enough water to just cover the fruit and stir in the lemon juice. Cook the fruit over a medium heat for approximately 20 minutes until soft.

3 Pour the fruit and juice through a damp cloth, retaining the juice. Weigh the juice, then boil together with the same amount of jam sugar until the set point is reached. Fill perfectly clean jars with the boiling hot mixture and seal straightaway. Store the jars in a cool place.

GOOSEBERRY JELLY

Makes 10 225 ml/8 fl oz jars

2 kg/4 lb 7 oz green gooseberries
1 vanilla pod
1.5 kg/3 lb 5 oz sugar
1 small bottle liquid pectin

1 Wash and clean the gooseberries, then place them in a steam juicer and cook. Measure out 1.5 1/2 pints 13 fl oz of juice and pour into a pan.

2 Slit the vanilla pod lengthways and scrape out the pulp. Add both the pod and the mark, as well as the sugar, to the juice.

3 Stirring continuously, bring the juice to the boil. Stir in the pectin and bring once more to the boil. Remove the vanilla pod. Pour the hot jelly into clean jars and seal them immediately.

SWEET AND SOUR CHERRY COMPOTE

Makes 3 500 ml/18 fl oz jars

1.5 kg/3 lb 5 oz black cherries
300 g/10½ oz sugar
125 ml/4½ fl oz wine vinegar
1 clove
½ cinnamon stick

1 Wash and stone the cherries, saving the juice. Mix together the sugar and vinegar, 125 ml/4½ fl oz

cherry juice (topped up with water if needed), the clove and cinnamon stick and bring to the boil.

2 Add the cherries and bring to the boil again. Lift out the cherries with a skimmer and distribute them in clean jars. Pour the liquid through a sieve on top. Close the jars tightly, and boil in a preserving pan for approximately 25 minutes at 80 °C/176 °F.

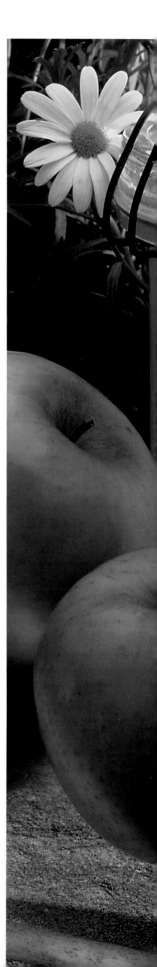

APRICOT AND LEMON BALM JAM

Tip

If apricot schnapps is too strong for your palette, an apricot liqueur can be used instead. This gives the preserve a gentler flavour.

Makes 7 230 ml/8 fl oz jars

1 kg/2¼ lb apricots (stoned weight)
1 kg/2¼ lb jam sugar 1:1
½ pot lemon balm
1 lime
40 ml/1½ fl oz apricot brandy
or apricot schnapps

1 Wash and stone the apricots. Chop the fruit into small pieces and combine with the jam sugar in a large pan.

2 Pluck the lemon balm leaves and chop finely. Rinse the lime in hot water, then cut the rind into thin strips with a zester and add to the apricots.

3 Bring the fruit mixture to a rolling boil for 4 minutes, stirring all the time. Then remove the pan from the heat and add the chopped lemon balm and apricot brandy.

4 Finally, rinse the twist-off jars with hot water and fill them immediately with the mixture, seal tightly, and stand upside down for 5 minutes. Turn the jars often during cooling to ensure the lemon balm is well distributed in the jam.

RHUBARB AND APPLE JAM

Tip

To save time, the fruit can be pureed with a hand blender as it cooks. That eliminates the need to let the mixture stand beforehand.

Makes 6 230 ml/8 fl oz jars

600 g/1 lb 5 oz rhubarb (weight when
    cleaned and prepared)
400 g/14 oz apples (weight when
    cleaned and prepared)
1 vanilla pod
1 large pinch ground coriander
1/2 tsp cinnamon
500 g/1 lb 2 oz jam sugar 2:1

1 Peel the rhubarb and the apples, remove the apple cores, and chop both into small cubes.

2 Slit the vanilla pod lengthways and scrape out the mark. Mix the vanilla pod, mark and other spices with the fruit cubes and jam sugar. Let stand for 1 to 2 hours.

3 Then bring the mixture to a rolling boil for 4 minutes, stirring occasionally.

4 Remove the vanilla pod and immediately fill twist-off jars that have been rinsed in hot water with the mixture. Seal the jars tightly, and before storing away stand them upside down for 5 minutes.

35

STEWED & PRESERVED FRUIT

PEARS WITH GINGER

Makes 2 500 ml/18 fl oz jars

1 kg/2¹/₄ lb pears
50 ml/1³/₄ fl oz dry white wine
2 Tbsp lemon juice
250 g/9 oz sugar
3–4 whole cloves
2 tsp ginger pieces
1 large pinch citric acid
¹/₂ tsp nutmeg
1 tsp ground cinnamon

1 Peel and halve the pears, remove the cores and cut into wedges.

2 Bring 200 ml/7 fl oz of water, the white wine, lemon juice, sugar, cloves and ginger pieces to the boil, and simmer at low heat for roughly 10 minutes. Stir in the citric acid and season the pears with the nutmeg and cinnamon.

3 Fill the prepared jars with the pear mixture, seal well and leave to stand in a cool place for approximately 12 hours.

Tip

Try the ginger pears with a dollop of vanilla cream—simply delicious!

MELON BALLS WITH ARRACK

Makes 1 rum pot or 1 tall jar

1 Galia melon (approx. 600 g/1 lb 5 oz)
2 untreated oranges
50 g/1³/₄ oz honey
500 ml/18 fl oz arrack (liqueur)
3–4 Tbsp lemon juice

1 Halve the melon, remove the seeds, and cut out the flesh with a melon scoop. Wash the oranges in hot water and cut into slices with the peel. Layer both fruits in a bowl.

2 Warm the honey. Add the arrack and the lemon juice. Stir well and pour over the fruit.

3 Cover the bowl and leave to stand in a cool place for 3 to 4 days. The preserved melon balls will keep for approximately 6 weeks. They are especially delicious when served with vanilla ice cream or whipped cream.

39

STEWED PLUMS AND GREENGAGES

Makes 6 500 ml/18 fl oz jars

2 kg/4½ lb plums
1 kg/2¼ lb greengages
500 g/1 lb 2 oz sugar
2 cinnamon sticks
1 tsp cloves
40 ml/1½ fl oz slivovitz (plum brandy)

1 Wash and stone the fruit. Boil up 1 litre/1¾ pints of water with the sugar, cinnamon sticks and cloves. Add the fruit and boil for a further 5 minutes. Remove any foam with a skimmer. Stir in the slivovitz.

2 Remove the fruit with a skimmer, filling the preserving jars. Top up with the cooking fluid, dividing the cloves and cinnamon between the jars. Seal the jars and cook in a preserving pan for 30 minutes at 80 °C/176 °F.

PEARS IN RED WINE

Makes 2
750 ml/1 pint 7 fl oz jars

1.2 kg/2 lb 10 oz pears (not too ripe)
4 Tbsp lemon juice
0.7 l/1$^{1}/_{4}$ pints dry red wine
150 g/5 oz sugar
1 cinnamon stick
4 cloves
1 bottle of citric acid (preserving aid)

1 Wash, dry, halve, core and peel the pears. Dribble lemon juice over them to prevent discolouring.

2 Heat the red wine together with 50 g/1$^{3}/_{4}$ oz sugar, the cinnamon stick and the cloves. Place the pear halves in the wine and briefly bring to the boil. Leave to stand for roughly 6 to 8 minutes.

3 Sprinkle the remaining sugar into the liquid and stir well. Stir in the preserving aid, following the directions for use. Fill the well rinsed jars with the mixture while still hot, and seal immediately.

41

CANDIED CHERRIES

Makes 4 500 ml/18 fl oz jars

1 kg/2¼ lb sweet cherries
      (alternatively sour cherries)
1 kg/2¼ lb sugar
200 ml/7 fl oz apple juice

1 Wash, stone and weigh the cherries. In a large bowl, make alternating layers of fruit and sugar, and allow to stand for 12 hours.

2 Boil the resulting juice in a large pan, stirring and occasionally skimming, until it becomes a thin syrup. Pour the boiling hot syrup over the fruit and leave to stand for a further 24 hours.

3 Drain the syrup once again, combine it with the apple juice, and reduce by a quarter. Once again, pour over the cherries while still boiling hot. Then allow the cherries to stand for 2 days.

4 Repeat step 3 another 2 to 3 times (without adding additional apple juice). Finally, fill the jars with the cooled cherries and seal airtight.

Tip
Candied cherries are known as Amarena cherries in Italian cuisine, and are the crowning touch on (almost) every portion of vanilla ice cream.

PRESERVED LEMONS

Makes 3 500 ml/18 fl oz jars

2¹/₂ kg/4 lb untreated lemons
500 g/1 lb 2 oz coarse salt
100 ml/3¹/₂ fl oz vegetable oil

1 Wash the lemons in hot water and rub dry. Slice them into quarters lengthways, taking care not to cut all the way through the peel. Carefully open up the lemons and sprinkle liberally with salt. Press the lemons together again to prevent the salt from falling out.

2 Rinse the jars with hot water, and carefully layer the lemons in them. Press the fruit down well, cover with cling-film, and weigh down with a stone or heavy container.

3 After 3 to 4 days, or when the lemons have leached enough juice to cover themselves completely, remove the stone, close the jars, and shake well to distribute the juice.

4 Top up the jars with oil, seal, and store in a cool place for 3 weeks.

Tip

In Moroccan cuisine, these lemons are used as an ideal accompaniment to well-spiced meat dishes, highly regarded for their sour, sharp and refreshing taste.

QUINCES AND FIGS IN SYRUP

Makes 2 500 ml/18 fl oz jars

For the quinces:
2 large quinces (approx. 800 g/1³/₄ lb)
Juice of 1 lemon
4 cloves
200 g/7 oz sugar
1 green apple

For the figs:
500 g/1 lb 2 oz fresh figs, not quite ripe
Juice of 2 lemons
500 g/1 lb 2 oz sugar
1 cinnamon stick

Tip
This is a dish straight from A Thousand and One Arabian Nights! Quinces and figs can be served with cheese. The sweet oriental note of the preserved fruit wonderfully complements the savoury aroma of the cheese.

1 Wash and peel the quinces, then cut them lengthways into eighths. Remove the cores, retaining 7–8 pips. Place the quinces, side by side, in a large pan and pour the lemon juice over them.

2 In order to make the syrup, add the cloves, the quince pips, the sugar and 500 ml/18 fl oz water to the pan. Peel the apple and grate it over the quinces. Cover the pan and cook the quinces for about 1¹/₂ hours or until they are soft to the touch. Occasionally baste with the sugar syrup.

3 Remove the quinces from the pan and place in a jar. Boil the syrup for about 10 minutes until it becomes a jelly. Remove the cloves and pips. Pour the syrup over the quinces and seal the jar tightly.

4 Wash, dry and cut the figs into quarters or eighths, according to size. Sprinkle with lemon juice and leave to stand. Then place the fruit, sugar and cinnamon stick in a pan with a little water and simmer for 15 minutes.

5 Shake the pan gently every now and then, but do not stir as the fruit will easily fall apart. Fill the rinsed jar with the cooled figs and close tightly.

SAFFRON PEARS IN WHITE WINE

Tip
The addition of ascorbic acid prevents the pears from turning brown.

Makes 2 1 litre/1³/₄ pint jars

1.75 kg/4 lb ripe, firm pears (about 8)
2 Tbsp vinegar
Water for topping up

For the liquor:
250 ml/9 fl oz dry white wine
Juice and peel of 1 untreated lemon
1 small jar of saffron
2 cinnamon sticks
8 cloves
2 Tbsp liquid sweetener
1 large pinch ascorbic acid

1 Peel the pears and cut in half. Cut out the cores with a melon scoop, and remove the stems and woody bottoms.

2 Place the fruit in a bowl with the vinegar and top up with enough water to cover the pears.

3 To make the liquor, boil up the white wine, lemon peel and juice, and spices. Add the pears and allow to stand for 5 to 8 minutes.

4 Layer the pears with the cinnamon sticks and cloves in thoroughly rinsed jars.

5 Top up the liquor with roughly 500 ml/18 fl oz of water and bring to the boil. Stir in the ascorbic acid, then pour the liquid over the pears and seal the jars straightaway.

KUMQUATS IN SYRUP

Makes 4 1 litre/1³/₄ pint jars
or 8 500 ml/18 fl oz jars

1 kg/2¹/₄ lb kumquats
2 kg/4¹/₂ lb extra coarse preserving sugar
500 ml/18 fl oz water
0.7 l/1¹/₄ pints white rum (54% alc. vol.)

1 Wash the kumquats and dry thoroughly. Prick each fruit all round or cut into thin slices.

2 Add the preserving sugar to the water and, while stirring, boil until the sugar has dissolved completely. Add the kumquats to the sugar solution and simmer for 5 to 6 minutes. Remove the pan from the heat and allow the kumquats to cool in the syrup.

3 Remove the fruit and place it in one large jar or several smaller ones. Pour the syrup and the rum over the kumquats, ensuring that the fruit is covered with liquid. Store in a cool, dark place for 4 weeks before consumption.

ORANGE PEEL IN SYRUP

Make 2 500 ml/18 fl oz jars

8 untreated oranges
    (approx. 1 kg/2¼ lb)
1 kg/2¼ lb sugar
Juice of 1 lemon

1 Wash the oranges in hot water and rub dry. Cut each fruit into 6 wedges and carefully remove the peel, laying it in a bowl of water. Then, using a needle, thread the peel onto kitchen string, allowing 10 pieces of peel per string until all the peel has been threaded. Knot the ends of the strings.

2 Soak the threaded peel in water for 24 hours, changing the water 3 or 4 times during this time. Then drain the peel and place in a pan with approximately 3 litres/5 pints of water. Bring it to the boil and simmer for 15 minutes. Drain the peel in a sieve.

3 Put the peel back in the pan and boil again in 3 litres/5 pints of water for 10 minutes, until the peel is soft but not mushy. Allow to drain for at least 1 hour.

4 Put the sugar and lemon juice in a pan with 150 ml/¼ pint of water. While stirring, bring to the boil to dissolve the sugar. Boil further until the solution has a syrupy consistency. Add the orange peel to the syrup after removing it from the strings. Simmer for 5 minutes, then leave the peel to stand in the syrup overnight.

5 The next day, heat up the syrup and peel mixture and cook to thicken for 4 minutes. Leave to cool, and then fill into jars rinsed in hot water. The orange peel will keep for about 10 months when stored in a cool, dry place.

Tip

For a simple yet delectable dessert, cut some of the orange peels into fine pieces and stir them with a little of the syrup into creamy quark or fromage blanc.

PRESERVED VEGETABLES

MARINATED MIXED VEGETABLES

Makes 2 500 ml/18 fl oz jars

750 g/1 lb 11 oz mixed vegetables
      (peppers, carrot, leek,
      mushrooms, fennel, cauliflower)
125 ml/4½ fl oz white wine
125 ml/4½ fl oz vinegar
100 ml/3½ fl oz olive oil
2 cloves garlic
1 tsp peppercorns
1 Tbsp coriander seeds
3 bay leaves
1 pinch sugar
Salt

1 Clean and peel the carrots. Wash and clean the other vegetables. Cut the peppers into wide slices, the carrot into slices of 0.5 cm/⅙ in. Slice the leek into 5 cm/2 in pieces, the mushrooms and fennel into thin strips. Split the cauliflower into florets.

2 Add the wine, vinegar and oil to 500 ml/18 fl oz of water in a sufficiently large pan. Peel the garlic cloves and use a garlic press to press them into the pan. Coarsely crush the peppercorns and coriander seeds and together with the bay leaves, sugar and salt, also add to the pan.

3 Bring the mixture to the boil and add the vegetables. Let it boil vigorously for about 15 minutes, then fill the well rinsed jars with the vegetables and seal tightly. The vegetables will keep in the refrigerator for approximately 3 weeks.

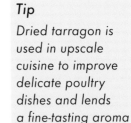

VEGETABLES WITH
MUSTARD AND TARRAGON

Makes 6–7 450 ml/16 fl oz jars

750 g/1 lb 11 oz each: cauliflower
      and broccoli
500 g/1 lb 2 oz each: shallots, cherry
      tomatoes and carrots
1 bunch tarragon
5 l/9 pints water
Salt
250 ml/9 fl oz vinegar essence (25%)
2 Tbsp mustard powder
1 l/1¾ pints cider
200 g/7 oz sugar
1 Tbsp mustard seeds
1 heaped Tbsp cornflour
2 Tbsp Dijon mustard

1 Separate the cauliflower and broccoli florets, peel the stems and cut lengthways into 5 mm/¹⁄₆ in slices. Wash the cherry tomatoes. Peel and, if necessary, halve the shallots and carrots. Pluck the tarragon leaves from their stalks and chop.

2 Bring the salted water to the boil over high heat. Except for the tomatoes, boil the vegetables a portion at a time until al dente, removing them with a skimmer and draining. Then layer the vegetables and the tomatoes in the prepared jars.

3 Mix the vinegar essence with the mustard powder. Bring to the boil with the cider, sugar and mustard seeds. Bind the liquid with the cornflour mixed in a little water, and add the tarragon and Dijon mustard.

4 Pour the boiling hot liquid over the vegetables. Seal the jars tightly.

Tip
Dried tarragon is used in upscale cuisine to improve delicate poultry dishes and lends a fine-tasting aroma to mayonnaise and herbal sauces.

TUSCAN FENNEL

Tip

Adding some of the fennel greenery to the marinade will make the finished product even more aromatic.

Makes 4–5 500 ml/18 fl oz jars

8 small fennel bulbs (2 kg/4¹/₂ lb)
750 ml/1 pint 7 fl oz water
¹/₂ tsp salt
5 cloves garlic
5 small onions
500 ml/18 fl oz white wine vinegar
5 Tbsp white wine
2 heaped Tbsp sugar
1 tsp black peppercorns
125 ml/4¹/₂ fl oz virgin olive oil
1 or 2 sprigs rosemary

1 Clean, wash and halve the fennel bulbs lengthways. Bring the water and salt to the boil, and cook the fennel bulbs in it for 8 to 10 minutes.

Measure out 500 ml/18 fl oz of the cooking liquid and set it aside.

2 Peel the garlic cloves and the onions, then place in the prepared jars together with the fennel. Bring the fennel cooking water, the white wine vinegar, white wine, sugar and the peppercorns to the boil.

3 Stir in the olive oil, then pour over the fennel in the jars. Add the sprigs of rosemary to the jars and seal. The next day, drain the liquid and bring it to the boil. After it has cooled pour it over the fennel once again. Seal the jars tightly. Store in a cool, dark place.

TANGY GARLIC GHERKINS

Makes 3 1 litre/1³/₄ pint jars

2 red peppers
1.5 kg/3 lb 5 oz small pickling cucumbers
     (gherkins)
200 g/7 oz red onions
16 cloves garlic (approx. 80 g/2³/₄ oz)
1 l/1³/₄ pints wine vinegar (6%)
400 g/14 oz sugar
4 Tbsp salt
1 Tbsp mustard seeds
¹/₂ packet pickling spices for gherkins
1 packet (=2.5 g/1 scant level tsp)
     ascorbic acid

1 Halve and clean out the red peppers, then thoroughly wash them and the gherkins.

2 Peel the onions and the cloves of garlic. Cut the garlic cloves in half, the onions into wedges, the cucumbers into slices and the peppers into cubes.

3 Bring the vinegar to the boil and add the sugar, salt, mustard seeds and pickling spices. Briefly blanch the vegetables in the liquor, remove and layer in the prepared jars.

4 Sprinkle the ascorbic acid in the gherkin water and dissolve. Pour the water over the vegetables to cover them completely.

5 Seal the jars well and leave to stand in a cool place for about a week.

ELEGANT VEGETABLE VARIATIONS

PEARL ONIONS IN RED WINE

Makes 1 500 ml/18 fl oz jar

500 g/1 lb 2 oz pearl onions
250 ml/9 fl oz water
1 level Tbsp salt

For the liquor:
500 ml/18 fl oz red wine
250 ml/9 fl oz red wine vinegar
1 level Tbsp salt
2-3 Tbsp liquid sweetener
1 tsp mustard seeds
8 allspice berries
2 bay leaves

1 Peel the onions. Salt the water and bring to the boil. Pour over the onions, covering them, and let stand overnight. The next day, drain well.

2 Bring all the ingredients for the liquor to the boil and cook for 3 minutes, then add the onions. Cook for a further 5 to 8 minutes until the onions are glassy but still firm.

3 Use a skimmer to transfer the onions to the prepared jar, then pour boiling hot liquor over them. Close the jar lid straightaway. The onions in red wine are ready to eat after 4 to 5 days.

SWEET CUCUMBER

Makes 2 500 ml/18 fl oz jars

1 kg/2¼ lb salad cucumbers
40 g/1½ oz salt

For the liquor:
250 ml/9 fl oz herbal vinegar
1½–2 Tbsp liquid sweetener
1 tsp mustard seeds
1 Tbsp pickling spice
1 bay leaf

1 Peel, halve and remove the seeds from the cucumber. Rub with the salt and leave to stand, covered, for 12 hours. Rinse with water several times, then dab dry.

2 Bring all the ingredients for the liquor to the boil. Halve the cucumbers again, and allow to soak briefly in the liquor. Then remove and pack, standing tightly together, in the hotly rinsed jars.

3 Boil up the liquor once again, and while still hot pour it over the cucumbers. Seal the lids of the jars immediately.

MARINATED ASPARAGUS

Makes a 1 litre/1³/₄ pint jar

1 kg/2¹/₄ lb white asparagus
500 ml/18 fl oz water
1–1¹/₂ Tbsp salt
250 ml/9 fl oz white wine vinegar
3 tsp liquid sweetener
1 tsp black peppercorns
1 tsp tarragon
1 tsp dill
1 tsp chervil

1 Peel the asparagus. Boil the peelings for about 15 minutes in salted water. Drain the liquor through a sieve, then mix together with the vinegar, liquid sweetener and peppercorns, and heat.

2 Cook the asparagus in this liquor for 5 minutes. Carefully remove it and stand upright in a well rinsed twist-off jar. Add the herbs.

3 Boil up the liquor once again, and pour over the asparagus while still hot. Seal the jar's lid immediately and allow to cool.

SWEET AND SOUR TOMATOES

Makes 3 250 ml/9 fl oz jars

1 kg/2¼ lb tomatoes, not too ripe
375 ml/13 fl oz wine vinegar
500 g/1 lb 2 oz preserving sugar
6 cloves
2 Tbsp coriander
1 cinnamon stick
2 onions
Juice and peel of 1 untreated lemon
½ Tbsp salt

1 Rinse the tomatoes and remove the stalk eyes. Pour the wine vinegar over them and leave, covered, to stand overnight.

2 The next day, drain the vinegar into a pan, and bring to the boil together with the sugar and spices.

3 Peel the onions and coarsely chop them. Boil up the chopped onions, a portion at a time, in the sugar-vinegar solution. Then layer the tomatoes and onions in the jars.

4 Pour the hot sugar-vinegar solution over the tomatoes, covering them.

5 Seal the jars and store in a cool, dark place.

PICKLED COURGETTE STRIPS WITH CHERRY TOMATOES

Makes 2 500 ml/18 fl oz jars

600 g/1 lb 5 oz courgettes
300 g/10½ oz cherry tomatoes
100 ml/3½ fl oz white wine vinegar
2 sprigs thyme
4 cloves garlic
10 white peppercorns
1 tsp salt
1 tsp ground ginger
1 Tbsp honey
Olive oil for topping up

1 Wash the courgettes, halve them and cut into strips. Clean the cherry tomatoes and prick all around with a toothpick. Peel and halve the garlic cloves.

2 Simmer the courgettes for about 3 minutes together with the vinegar, thyme, garlic, peppercorns, salt, ground ginger and honey.

3 Allow to cool and then put into the prepared jars. Add the tomatoes and top up with olive oil.

4 Seal the jars and leave to stand in a cool place for about 3 days. The jars will keep for 3 months or even longer. The pickled courgettes should not be served too cold. Their aroma is best at room temperature.

HEARTY VEGETABLE VARIATIONS

BROAD BEANS WITH SAGE

Makes 3–4 500 ml/18 fl oz jars

100 ml/3½ fl oz vinegar essence (25%)
1 l/1¾ pints water
1 tsp salt
1 Tbsp sugar
1 tsp mustard seeds
1 kg/2¼ lb broad beans (shelled weight)
100 g/3½ oz pearl onions
12 sage leaves

1 Boil together the vinegar essence, water, salt, sugar and mustard seeds. Simmer the broad beans and peeled pearl onions in the liquid for about 10 minutes.

2 Remove the beans and onions and place them, with the sage leaves, in jars rinsed with hot water. Boil the liquid for a further 5 minutes then pour over the beans. Seal the jars well and store in a cool and dark place.

COLOURFUL SOUR MIXED PEPPERS

Makes 4 1 litre/1¾ pint jars

2 kg/4½ lb green, red and yellow
        peppers
3–4 medium-sized onions
150 ml/¼ pint vinegar essence (25%)
1 l/1¾ pints water
1 tsp salt
2 tsp sugar
1 Tbsp black peppercorns

1 Cut the peppers in half lengthways. Remove the stem tops and seeds. Lay the halves skin up on an oven rack and bake for 20 minutes at 220 °C/390 °F/gas mark 6 (convector oven: 180 °C/355 °F/gas mark 4) until the skin blisters.

2 In the meantime, peel the onions and cut into thin slices. Remove the peppers from the oven and pull off the skin. Layer the skinned peppers in the prepared jars.

3 Bring the vinegar essence, water, spices and onion slices to the boil, then pour over the peppers. Close the jars. After 2 days, drain off the liquid and bring to the boil. Allow to cool, then once again pour over the peppers. Close the jars immediately.

SWEET AND SOUR CAULIFLOWER

Makes 1 500 ml/18 fl oz jar

1 medium-sized cauliflower
Salt
3 onions
3 cloves garlic
1 untreated lemon
2 star aniseeds
2 dried chillies
1 Tbsp peppercorns
375 ml/13 fl oz vinegar
125 g/4½ oz sugar

1 Clean the cauliflower, cut it into florets and cook in salted water for about 10 minutes. Remove, drain, allow to cool and place the florets in a sufficiently large preserving jar.

2 Peel and finely chop the onions and the cloves of garlic. Rub the lemon with a dry cloth and cut into slices. Spread the onions, garlic, lemon slices, star aniseed, chillies and peppercorns over the cauliflower florets.

3 Bring the vinegar, sugar and 500 ml/18 fl oz water to the boil, and pour over the cauliflower. Leave to cool, then seal the jar. Let the cauliflower stand for at least 12 hours before eating.

MARINATED OLIVES

Makes 3 500 ml/18 fl oz jars of each kind of olives

Marinade I:
2 cloves garlic
1 Tbsp chopped oregano
Grated peel of ½ untreated orange
1 l/1¾ pints olive oil
1 tsp dried chilli flakes
500 g/1 lb 2 oz green olives

Marinade II:
2 cloves garlic
1 Tbsp chopped oregano
1 tsp ground cumin
1 l/1¾ pints olive oil
1 tsp dried chilli flakes
500 g/1 lb 2 oz black olives

1 Peel the garlic cloves and finely chop them.

2 Mix all the ingredients for the first marinade together with the green olives.

3 Mix all the ingredients for the second marinade together with the black olives.

4 Put each type of olive in a different lidded jar and seal tightly.

Tip
Olives are wonderfully suited as a simple accompaniment for wine and cheese, but are also often found in rustic salads and as a garnish all around the Mediterranean basin.

ONIONS IN SHERRY

Makes 3 500 ml/18 fl oz jars

1 kg/2¼ lb small onions
    (pearl onions)
200 ml/7 fl oz sherry vinegar
10 g/¼ oz salt
200 g/7 oz sugar
4 bay leaves
6 fresh sage leaves
4 cloves
10 black peppercorns
Thinly peeled rind of 1 untreated lemon
Roughly 250 ml/9 fl oz dry sherry

1 Peel the onions and simmer in water for 10 minutes. Remove and drain well. Bring the vinegar, salt and half of the sugar to the boil, add the onions, herbs and spices, and allow to cool in the liquid. Then remove the onions, reserving the liquor.

2 Caramelise the remaining sugar in a pan, stirring constantly. Remove the pan from the heat and add the sherry-vinegar solution, stirring until the caramel dissolves. Add the onions and spices to the liquid. Cook for 5 minutes, then remove from the heat.

3 Add the sherry to the liquid. Remove the onions and spices and put into jars. Pour the hot liquid over them, and seal with twist-off lids.

4 The onions will keep in the refrigerator for about 3 months. They are delicious with meat and game dishes.

PICKLED WHITE CABBAGE

Tip

Beetroot can also be pickled. To do so, thoroughly wash 700 g/1¹/₂ lb of the vegetable, clean with a brush and cut into thin slices. Peel 2 onions and cut into rings. Fill a large jar to ³/₄ full with the beetroot, onion, 1 tsp caraway, 1 bay leaf, ¹/₄ tsp dill seeds and a few tarragon leaves. Press together slightly. Boil up salted water (20 g/³/₄ oz salt per litre/1³/₄ pints of water) and pour enough over the vegetables to cover them well. Seal the jar and leave it in a dark place to ferment at room temperature for about a week. Then store in a cool place. The pickled beetroot is ready to eat after approximately 3 weeks, and should be consumed within a short period. Pickled beetroot cannot be kept too long as it becomes increasingly acidic.

Makes 2 1 litre/1³/₄ pint jars

1 medium-sized white cabbage
12 cloves garlic
1 Tbsp salt
1 l/1³/₄ pints white wine vinegar
4 small bay leaves

1 Remove the outer leaves from the head of cabbage. Cut it into four pieces, remove the hard inner stalk and chop the rest into thin strips.

2 Peel the garlic, crush in a mortar with the salt, then mix with the vinegar.

3 Press the strips of cabbage into the jars, then add half the vinegar mixture and 2 bay leaves to each jar. Top off with enough water to cover the cabbage.

4 Seal the jars and leave to stand in cool, dark place for 4 to 5 days. Store in a cool place.

COLOURFUL VEGETABLE VARIATIONS

PICKLED GREEN TOMATOES WITH CELERIAC

Makes 6 500 ml/18 fl oz jars

2.5 kg/5½ lb small green tomatoes
2 Tbsp iodised salt
1.5 l/2½ pints white wine vinegar
175 g/6 oz sugar
1 tsp black peppercorns
1 tsp fennel seeds
250 g/9 oz medium-sized onions
300 g/10½ oz celeriac

1 Gently wash the tomatoes. Prick them all around with a wooden skewer, sprinkle them with salt and leave to stand in a bowl at room temperature overnight.

2 The next day, top up the resulting liquid with water to 750 ml/1 pint 7 fl oz and bring to the boil in a pan together with the vinegar, sugar, peppercorns and fennel seeds.

3 Peel the onions and cut into slices. Peel the celeriac and cut first into slices, then into thin strips.

4 Layer the tomatoes, celeriac strips and sliced onions in jars previously rinsed with hot water, then fill with the liquid. Seal the jars and preserve in hot water for 30 minutes at 80 °C/ 176 °F.

COLOURFUL PICKLED VEGETABLES

Makes 4 1 litre/1¾ pint jars

500 g/1 lb 2 oz carrots
250 g/9 oz green beans
500 g/1 lb 2 oz celery
2 medium-sized fennel bulbs
2 red peppers
1 bunch spring onions
130 g/4½ oz salt
750 ml/1 pint 7 fl oz herbal vinegar
2 Tbsp mustard seeds
40 g/1½ oz ginger root
2 small bay leaves
3–4 Tbsp liquid sweetener

1 Wash and clean all the vegetables. Quarter the carrots, cut the celery and spring onions into pieces, the fennel into slices and the peppers into strips.

2 Bring 2 litres/3½ pints water to the boil. Add all but 10 g of the salt and successively cook the vegetables al dente. Remove and drain well.

3 Bring the vinegar, 500 ml/18 fl oz water, the remaining salt, the mustard seeds, ginger, bay leaves and the liquid sweetener to the boil.

4 Place alternating layers of vegetables in preserving jars, pour the liquid over them and seal the jars. Let stand overnight.

5 The next day, drain the liquid from the jars into a pan, reheat, and pour over the vegetables again. Seal the jars immediately and store in a cool, dark place.

DEVILISH CUCUMBERS

Tip
*Devilish cucumbers
are an ideal
accompaniment for
aspic dishes and
hearty fried pota-
toes. No picnic or
barbeque is truly
complete without
them.*

Makes 3 1 litre/1³/₄ pint jars

3 kg/6 lb 10 oz salad cucumbers
100 g/3¹/₂ oz salt
1 bunch lovage
¹/₂ horseradish root
4 cloves garlic
750 ml/1 pint 7 fl oz wine vinegar
750 ml/1 pint 7 fl oz white wine
750 ml/1 pint 7 fl oz water
2 Tbsp crushed black peppercorns
2 Tbsp green peppercorns
2 Tbsp mustard seeds
2 bay leaves
250 g/9 oz sugar

1 Peel the cucumber, cut lengthways and scrape out the seeds with a spoon. Cut the cucumber into pieces of equal size, put them in a bowl, salt liberally and leave to stand overnight.

2 The following day, rub the cucumbers dry with a clean cloth and place them into prepared preserving jars.

3 Trim the lovage. Clean, wash and peel the horseradish. Peel and chop the garlic.

4 In a pan, combine the wine vinegar, white wine and water. Add the lovage, horseradish, garlic, peppercorns, mustard seeds, bay leaves and sugar. Boil up the mixture, allow it to cool somewhat, then pour over the cucumber.

5 Seal the jars tightly with cling film, parchment paper or best of all with a lid, and leave to stand for at least a week.

AUBERGINES IN SYRUP

Makes 2 500 ml/18 fl oz jars

1 kg/2¹/₄ lb aubergines
Juice of 2 lemons
2 cinnamon sticks
350 g/12 oz sugar
5 cloves

1 Wash and clean the aubergines. Soak them in water and the juice of 1 lemon overnight. Then bring the aubergines and lemon water to the boil and simmer for approximately 15 minutes until soft. Remove from the pan and leave to cool.

2 Bring 500 ml/18 fl oz of water to the boil with the cinnamon sticks, then simmer over a low heat for about 30 minutes. Add the sugar, stirring all the while until the sugar has dissolved.

3 Add the aubergines to the sugar solution and simmer for about 10 minutes. Remove the pan from the heat, cover and leave to stand overnight.

4 The next day, slowly reheat the aubergines in the syrup, add the remaining lemon juice and cloves, and cook until the syrup thickens.

5 Rinse out 2 preserving jars with hot water and fill with the aubergines in syrup. Seal the jars well and let the aubergines to stand for about 3 weeks before eating.

Tip
Aubergines and feta cheese tidbits complement each other well, and are a decorative part of every Mediterranean starter buffet.

PRESERVED CELERY

Makes 2 250 ml/9 fl oz jars

1 celery with leaves
1 fennel bulb with greenery
100 ml/3¹/₂ fl oz olive oil
Juice of 2 lemons
2 tsp fresh chopped dill
2 bay leaves
Salt
Black pepper

1 Clean and wash the celery, then cut it into 4 cm/1¹/₂ in pieces. Clean, wash, dry and cut the fennel into small pieces.

2 Heat the oil in a pan. Briefly sweat the fennel, lemon juice, dill and bay leaves, add 100 ml/3¹/₂ fl oz of water and bring to the boil. Season with salt and pepper.

3 Add the celery to the liquid and pour on enough water to cover everything. Weigh down the celery with a plate and cook over a low heat for about 10 minutes. Remove from the heat and allow to cool.

4 Fill rinsed, screw-on-lid jars with the vegetables, cover with the liquid and seal. Leave to stand for about 3 weeks. The celery tastes especially good with cold meat or as a starter.

SWEET AND SOUR PUMPKIN

Makes 5–6 250 ml/9 fl oz jars

300 g/10½ oz prunes
250 ml/9 fl oz Armagnac
1 piece root ginger (approx. 20 g/¾ oz)
750 g/1 lb 11 oz small onions
1 pumpkin (about 1.2 kg/2¾ lb)
375 ml/13 fl oz white wine
375 ml/13 fl oz white wine vinegar
500 g/1 lb 2 oz soft honey
5 bay leaves

1 Soak the prunes in the Armagnac, covered, overnight.

2 Peel the ginger and cut into thin slices. Peel the pumpkin, remove the seeds and white fibres, and cube the flesh. Peel the onions.

3 Bring the white wine, vinegar, honey, bay leaves and ginger to the boil in a pan, then add the onions and simmer over a low heat for about 20 minutes. Remove the onions with a skimmer and put to one side.

4 Add the pumpkin to the liquid for about 5 minutes until glassy. When making large amounts, cook a portion at a time.

5 Layer the pumpkin, onions and prunes in well rinsed jars. Stir the Armagnac into the liquid and pour into the jars. Seal the jars and leave to stand for approximately 1 week. The sweet and sour pumpkin will keep for 4 to 6 months in a cool place.

Tip

Sweet and sour pumpkin is a traditional accompaniment for turkey and is a must for every American Thanksgiving meal.

PUMPKIN COMPOTE WITH CALVADOS

Tip

To make pumpkin compote without the apple, double the amount of pumpkin and cook slightly longer, for about 7 minutes.

Makes 6 230 ml/8 fl oz jars

1 pumpkin (approx. 500 g/1 lb 2 oz)
500 g/1 lb 2 oz Boskop apples
1 kg/2¼ lb jam sugar
Juice of 1 lemon
20 ml/4 tsp Calvados or grappa

1 Peel the pumpkin, remove the seeds and white fibres, and cube the flesh. Peel the apples, remove the cores and dice the flesh.

2 Combine the pumpkin and apple cubes, the jam sugar and lemon juice in a pan and cook for about 5 minutes while stirring.

3 Remove the pan from the heat and stir in the Calvados. Fill twist-off jars that have been rinsed in hot water with the compote, seal and stand upside down until set.

PICKLED CARROTS

Makes 3 450 ml/16 fl oz jars

1 kg/2¼ lb small carrots
3 cloves garlic
1 bunch fresh parsley, chopped
2 untreated lemons
1 Tbsp sugar
250 ml/9 fl oz vinegar

1 Wash, trim and peel the carrots and cut lengthways. When removing the greenery, leave a little remaining on the carrots. Alternatively, cut the carrots into slices.

2 Cook the carrots in boiling salt water for 2 to 3 minutes until al dente. Drain, reserving the liquid, rinse in cold water and leave to drain on a kitchen cloth.

3 Weigh down the carrots with a heavy object, e.g. a chopping board, but do not crush them. Peel and slice the garlic. Rinse the lemons in hot water and cut into slices.

4 Layer the carrots, garlic and parsley in a large jar with a screw-on lid. Lay the lemon slices on top, fill up with equal amounts of vinegar and the salt water and seal the jar. Place the jar in a warm, dark place for about a week before eating.

Tip
The same recipe can also be used for green beans; however, beans should not be weighted down.

COLOURFUL MIXED PEPPERS

Makes 2–3 450 ml/16 fl oz jars

500 g/1 lb 2oz each: red and
            yellow peppers
1–2 tsp salt
250 g/9 oz spring onions
2 cloves garlic
2 bay leaves
20 black peppercorns
6 Tbsp vinegar essence (25%)

1 Clean, wash and cut the peppers
  into quarters or eighths. Boil them
in lightly salted water, rinse in cold
water and drain (reserve the cooking
liquid). Clean, wash and cut the spring
onions into diagonal slices of 3 to
4 cm/1–1½ in.

2 Prepare the jars and fill with the
  spring onions, peppers, sliced garlic, bay leaves and peppercorns. Top
up the cooking liquid with the vinegar
essence and water to make 800 ml/
1 pint 8 fl oz and pour over the vegetables to cover them.

3 Wet rubber rings and place on the
  jars, close the lids and seal with
clamps. Stand in a preserving pan
filled with enough water to ¾ cover
the jars. Close the pan and cook the
jars for 30 minutes at 100 °C/212 °F.

MÉNAGE À TROIS

**Makes 2 750 ml/
1 pint 7 fl oz jars**

2 large courgettes
3 large red peppers
250 g/9 oz shallots
Salt
6 pinches dill
8 bay leaves
2 tsp allspice
6 Tbsp mustard seeds
2 Tbsp black peppercorns
340 ml/12 fl oz fruit vinegar
260 g/9 oz sugar

1 Wash, clean and slice the courgettes about 5 mm/⅙ in thick. Trim the peppers and remove the seeds, wash and cut into rings.

2 Skin the shallots and cut in half. Blanch each vegetable separately in boiling salted water and layer alternating in the preserving jars.

3 Bring to the boil 200 ml/7 fl oz water with 4 tsp salt, the spices, the vinegar and sugar, simmer for 5 minutes, then pour over the vegetables. Allow the jars to cool, then seal and leave to stand for 24 to 48 hours.

Tip
This mildly savoury vegetable cocktail amazes with its brilliant, cheerful colours that conjure up the energy of summer even on a grey autumn day. Of course, the colours can be varied by using yellow instead of red peppers, which also provide an excellent contrast to the green of the courgettes.

HONEYED SHALLOTS IN RAPESEED OIL

Makes 2 jars

1 kg/2¹/₄ lb shallots
750 ml/1 pint 7 fl oz rapeseed oil
3 Tbsp rapeseed honey
1 glass white wine (150 ml/¹/₄ pint)
1 bunch fresh oregano
1 bunch fresh marjoram
Freshly ground white or black pepper

1 Peel the shallots and fry golden brown in 2 Tbsp of the rapeseed oil. Add the honey and cook for about 2 minutes. Stir in the white wine, cover and leave to stew for 5 minutes.

2 Pluck the herb leaves from the stems, carefully rinse and spin until dry, then add to the shallots. Season with pepper.

3 Allow the shallots to cool, then fill the jars. Top up with the remaining rapeseed oil and seal with the lids. The shallots will keep in a cool, dark place for about 3 weeks.

PICKLED PUMPKIN WITH COURGETTES

Makes 4–5 1 litre/1³/₄ pint jars

2 kg/4¹/₂ lb pumpkin
500 g/1 lb 2 oz courgettes
1.5 l/2¹/₂ pints water
150 ml/¹/₄ pint vinegar essence (25%)
4 Tbsp sugar
1 tsp salt
1 tsp mustard powder
10 cloves
1 Tbsp mustard seeds
2 sprigs fresh tarragon
Several dill blossoms

1 Slice the pumpkin into wedges, remove the seeds and peel, then cut the flesh into cubes. Clean, wash and cut the courgettes into thick slices.

2 Bring the water, vinegar essence and spices to the boil. Add the cubes of pumpkin and slices of courgette and cook until glassy. Fill the jars with the vegetables and dill blossoms. Pour the cooking liquid over the top, covering the contents completely.

3 Wet rubber rings and place on the jars, close the lids and seal with clamps. Stand in a preserving pan filled with enough water to ³/₄ cover the jars. Close the pan and cook the jars for 30 minutes at 90 °C/194 °F.

MUSHROOM, EGG
& CHEESE SPECIALITIES

PICKLED MUSHROOMS

Makes 2 500 ml/18 fl oz jars
With chilli:
1 kg/2¼ lb button mushrooms
1 bunch fresh thyme
2–3 chillies
250 ml/9 fl oz white wine vinegar
2 tsp mustard seeds
2 Tbsp sugar
1 tsp salt
4 Tbsp olive oil

Makes 2 500 ml/18 fl oz jars
With garlic:
1 kg/2¼ lb button mushrooms
3 cloves garlic
250 ml/9 fl oz white wine vinegar
1 tsp black peppercorns
1 small sprig rosemary
2 Tbsp sugar, 1 tsp salt
4 Tbsp olive oil

With chilli:

1 Dry-rub the mushrooms to clean. Pluck the thyme leaves. Cut the chillies into rings, removing the seeds. Bring the vinegar, spices and thyme to the boil, add the mushrooms and cook for a further 5 minutes.

2 Allow to cool in the liquid, then fill the jars and top up with olive oil.

With garlic:

1 Dry-rub the mushrooms to clean. Peel and slice the garlic. Bring the vinegar, spices and rosemary to the boil, add the mushrooms and cook for a further 5 minutes.

2 Allow to cool in the liquid, then fill the jars and top up with olive oil.

MUSHROOMS IN A GLASS

Makes 4–5 450 ml/16 fl oz jars

1 kg/2¼ lb mushrooms (not too large)
5 small shallots
3 cloves garlic
500 ml/18 fl oz herbal vinegar
250 ml/9 fl oz water
4 cloves
8 white peppercorns
1 small bay leaf
2 tsp salt
8 Tbsp olive oil

1 Clean the mushrooms, wash and dab dry. Peel the shallots and cloves of garlic. Bring the shallots, garlic, herbal vinegar, water and spices to the boil. Add the mushrooms to the boiling liquid and leave to stand for 8 to 10 minutes, according to size.

2 Layer the mushrooms, shallots and garlic in jars. Allow the liquid to cool, then pour over the mushrooms. Carefully top up with the olive oil. Seal the jars immediately and store in a cool place.

Tip
The aroma of these mushrooms is intensified if they are briefly warmed before serving.

81

DELICIOUS EGG SPECIALITIES

MARINATED EGGS

18 eggs
1 Tbsp iodised salt
1 l/1¾ pints white wine vinegar
1 Tbsp white peppercorns
1 Tbsp chopped ginger
1 tsp allspice berries
1 large bay leaf

1 Hard boil the eggs in lightly salted water. Immediately rinse them in cold running water and peel. Place in a tall, wide-necked jar.

2 Heat the vinegar and add the coarsely crushed peppercorns, chopped ginger, allspice berries, the coarsely crumbled bay leaf and the salt. Simmer everything for about 10 minutes, then let cool.

3 When the liquid is cool, pour over the eggs through a sieve. The liquid must completely cover the eggs.

4 Close the jar tightly and leave to stand in a cool, dark place for about 4 weeks. The eggs are then ready to be eaten.

YELLOW EGGS IN BRINE

2 large onions
The skins of 3 onions
1 Tbsp iodised salt
18 white eggs

1 Coarsely cut up the unpeeled onions. Boil them in a pan with roughly 2 litres/3½ pints of water, 1 tsp salt and the additional onion skins. Simmer for 10 minutes, then bring to the boil again and use to cook the eggs until hard.

2 Remove the eggs from the cooking liquid, rinse under cold running water and lightly crack the shells all around so that they are broken but do not fall off. Place the eggs in a wide-necked jar with a volume of about 2 litres/3½ pints.

3 Bring about 1.5 litres/2½ pints of water to the boil, add the remaining salt and dissolve. Allow the brine to cool, then pour it over the eggs.

4 Seal the jar tightly and allow the eggs to stand in the brine for at least 24 hours. The eggs are then ready to be enjoyed. They are traditionally eaten with vinegar, oil and mustard.

PICKLED LUXURY MUSHROOMS

Makes 2 500 ml/18 fl oz jars

1 kg/2¼ lb fresh yellow boletus mushrooms
Iodised salt
750 ml/1 pint 7 fl oz white wine vinegar
3 bay leaves
15 peppercorns
3 Tbsp sugar
100 ml/3½ fl oz olive oil

1 Thoroughly sort and clean the mushrooms, then slice and cook them in a little lightly salted water for about 15 minutes. Remove and drain well.

2 In a second pan, bring the vinegar, bay leaves, peppercorns and sugar to the boil. Fill clean jars with the mushrooms and top up with the hot vinegar. Leave to stand for at least 2 months before eating. The pickled mushrooms will keep for months.

MUSHROOMS IN OIL

2 500 ml/18 fl oz jars

1 kg/2¼ lb fresh mushrooms
4 onions
250 ml/9 fl oz raspberry vinegar
1 tsp each: sugar and salt
3 sprigs each: parsley,
      marjoram and thyme
1 jar olives stuffed with pimento
500 ml/18 fl oz soya oil

1 As far as possible, the mushrooms should be cleaned by rubbing with a cloth and not washing. Then cut them into slices. Peel the onions, cut into quarters or eighths. Combine the vinegar, seasonings and herbs, add the oinions, bring to the boil and pour over the mushrooms while still hot.

2 When cool add the olives and top up with soya oil until everything is covered. Store in a cool place.

Goat's Cheese in Oil

Makes 1 500 ml/18 fl oz jar

1 sprig rosemary

3 sprigs thyme

2 chillies

6 small goat's cheeses

2 bay leaves

3 allspice berries

10 green peppercorns in brine

10 pink peppercorns in brine

500 ml/18 fl oz virgin olive oil

1 Rinse the herbs and thoroughly dab them dry. Also wash and dry the chillies.

2 Layer the goat's cheeses, herbs and spices in a large jar and cover with olive oil.

3 Seal the jar tightly and leave to stand in a cool place for at least a week. The goat's cheese will keep for up to 4 weeks in the oil.

ANTIPASTI SANTA LUCIA

Serves 4

**2 mozzarella cheeses
        (125 g/4½ oz each)
100 g/3½ oz piquant pepperonis (jar)
1 red onion
100 g/3½ oz stoned black olives
1 bunch basil
1 bunch rocket
1 garlic clove
100 ml/3½ fl oz olive oil
6 Tbsp white balsamic vinegar
Salt
Ground mixed peppercorns**

1 Drain the mozzarella well and cut into coarse cubes. Remove the stalks from the pepperoni as desired and cut them into halves, according to size.

2 Peel the onions, cut into coarse cubes and mix together with the mozzarella, pepperoni and olives. Pluck the basil leaves and, together with the rocket, wash, dab dry and chop.

3 Peel and crush the garlic, mix with the olive oil and balsamic vinegar and season with salt and pepper. Stir in the herbs, mix with the antipasti and chill for 5 minutes. This dish is delicious with crusty ciabatta bread.

87

PIQUANT MUSHROOMS

Tip

These piquant mushrooms are delicious with grilled meat, savoury pastries and fish. They also make an excellent starter and are a good eye-catcher on a cold buffet.

Makes 2 500 ml/18 fl oz jars

500 g/1 lb 2 oz mushrooms
4 onions
250 ml/9 fl oz white wine
250 ml/9 fl oz fruit vinegar
1 l/1³/₄ pints water
250 g/9 oz sugar
2 Tbsp peppercorns
2 Tbsp mustard seeds
1 Tbsp juniper berries
1 Tbsp salt
1 bunch tarragon

1 Clean and wash the mushrooms, then boil briefly in salted water. Peel an dslice the onions.

2 Heat white wine, vinegar, water, sugar, peppercorns, mustard seeds, juniper berries and salt in a pan. Add the onions and simmer for 5 minutes.

3 Divide the well-drained mushrooms between the jars, cover with the hot liquid and leave to cool. When cold, seal the jars and leave to stand for at least 10 days before eating.

MUSHROOMS WITH ROSEMARY

Makes 1 500 ml/18 fl oz jar

600 g/1 lb 5 oz small mushrooms
1 sprig rosemary
5 juniper berries
2 Tbsp mixed peppercorns
1 bay leaf
1 tsp salt
1 tsp sugar
100 ml/3½ fl oz white wine vinegar
Olive oil for topping up

1 Trim, rub and if necessary wash and rub dry the mushrooms.

2 Bring the vinegar to the boil with the rosemary, juniper berries, pepper, bay leaf, salt and sugar. Add the mushrooms and cook for about 3 minutes.

3 Let the mushrooms cool in the cooking liquid, then pour into a prepared glass jar (never use a plastic container), and top up with olive oil.

4 Seal the jar well and leave to stand for about 3 days.

LIVELY CHEESE SPECIALITIES

FIERY FETA

Makes 1 2 litre/3¹/₂ pint jar

500 g/1 lb 2 oz Feta (sheep's cheese)
juice of 1 lemon
2 Tbsp hot paprika powder
1 tsp cayenne pepper
1.5 l/2¹/₂ pints soya oil

1 Cut the feta into cubes. Press the lemon and sprinkle the juice over the cheese, then put the cubes into a suitable container.

2 Carefully stir the paprika and cayenne pepper into the soya oil (do not whisk) and pour a drop at a time over the cheese. Store for 2 days in a cool, dark place.

SAVOURY GOAT'S CHEESE

Makes 1 2 litre/3¹/₂ pint jar

1 fresh bulb garlic
500 g/1 lb 2 oz roll goat's cheese
1 small jar capers
1.5 l/2¹/₂ pints soya oil

1 Remove the outer skin from the garlic and cut the bulb into thin slices. Cut the cheese into finger-thick slices.

2 Put the garlic and cheese slices in a suitable container, add the capers and top up with the soya oil.

3 Leave to stand in a cool, dark place for 2 to 3 days.

AROMATIC ROQUEFORT CHEESE

Makes 1 2 litre/3¹/₂ pint jar

500 g/1 lb 2 oz Roquefort cheese
1 untreated orange
1 small bunch basil
1.5 l/2¹/₂ pints soya oil

1 Cut the cheese into slices. Thinly peel the orange. Rinse the basil and dab well until completely dry.

2 Put the ingredients into a suitable container and top up with the soya oil. Leave to stand for 2 to 3 days in a cool, dark place before eating.

GOAT'S CHEESE WITH CHILLI

Makes 2 250 ml/9 fl oz jars

300 g/10½ oz firm goat's cheese
2 chillies
1 sprig rosemary
2 small bay leaves
1 tsp mild paprika powder
2 cloves garlic
150 ml/¼ pint virgin olive oil

1 Cut the goat's cheese into cubes. Slightly slit the chillies. Pluck the rosemary leaves from the stem. Peel and halve the garlic cloves and evenly distribute all the ingredients into 2 prepared jars.

2 Add the paprika powder and bay leaves (one half in each jar) and top up with the olive oil.

3 Seal the jars tightly and rotate several times to make sure the ingredients are mixed together well. Leave to stand for at least 3 days. Unopened, the goat's cheese will keep for 3 to 6 months.

PICKLED PEPPERED CHEESE

Makes 1 2 litre/3½ pint jar

600 g/1 lb 5 oz cherry tomatoes
1 red chilli
6 cloves garlic
1 Tbsp vinegar
2 Tbsp sugar
2 tsp salt
1 bunch basil
1 bunch oregano
1 bunch thyme
300 g/10½ oz mozzarella
1 Tbsp mixed peppercorns

1 Wash the tomatoes and prick all around with a wooden skewer. Wash, clean and halve the chilli, remove the seeds and cut into pieces. Peel the cloves of garlic.

2 Bring 250 ml/9 fl oz water to the boil together with the vinegar, garlic, sugar and salt. Wash the herbs, shake dry and pluck off individual sprigs. Drain the mozzarella and cut into quarters.

3 Put the tomatoes, chilli pieces, mozzarella and herbs in a sealable jar and cover with the seasoned water. Add the peppercorns and allow to cool.

4 Seal the jar and leave to stand for about 12 hours in a cool place.

MARINATED MOZZARELLA BALLS

Tip

Mozzarella balls the size of quails' eggs are available in the shops. They are especially suitable for marinating in oil and lend a pretty appearance to the finished product.

Serves 4

1 sprig rosemary
1 sprig thyme
3 cloves garlic
150 g/5 oz cherry tomatoes
50 g/1¾ oz stuffed olives
150 g/5 oz mozzarella balls
Salt
Several white peppercorns
2 bay leaves
250 ml/9 fl oz olive oil

1 Wash and shake dry the herbs. Peel the garlic. Clean, wash and rub dry the tomatoes.

2 Cut the olives into slices. Drain the mozzarella balls. Combine everything, including the salt, peppercorns and bay leaves, in a preserving jar.

3 Top up with the oil, seal the jar and leave to stand for about 12 hours. Serve the mozzarella balls with fresh, crusty white bread.

MUSHROOMS IN WINE VINEGAR MARINADE

Makes 2 250 ml/9 fl oz jars

800 g/1³/₄ lb small mushrooms
1 l/1³/₄ pints meat stock
2 cloves garlic
2 bay leaves
5 sage leaves
1 tsp peppercorns
2 sprigs thyme
300 ml/10¹/₂ fl oz red wine vinegar
50 ml/1³/₄ fl oz olive oil
1 tsp salt

1 Rub the mushrooms clean without water and trim the stalks.

2 Heat the stock and blanch the mushrooms in it for a minute or so. Remove the mushrooms and place them in the prepared jars.

3 Add the herbs, peppercorns and salt to the jars.

4 Mix the vinegar and oil with a little of the stock, bring to the boil and pour over the mushrooms.

5 Seal the jars immediately and leave to stand for about 2 days. The mushrooms will keep for roughly 2 weeks.

95

CHUTNEYS, SEASONINGS & RELISHES

CHILLI AND MARROW CHUTNEY

Makes 2 1 litre/1³/₄ pint jars

1 kg/2¹/₄ lb marrow
250 g/9 oz shallots
20 g/³/₄ oz fresh root ginger
¹/₄ bunch dill
3 red chillies
200 ml/7 fl oz white wine vinegar
400 g/14 oz sugar
1 Tbsp mustard seeds
Salt
Freshly ground pepper

1 Wash and peel the marrow. Slice it lengthways and scrape out the seeds with a spoon. Cut the marrow first into 2 to 3 pieces and then into thin strips.

2 Peel the shallots and cut into cubes. Peel and grate the ginger. Wash the dill, shake dry and finely chop. Wash, dry and halve the chillies, remove the seeds and cut into strips.

3 Bring 200 ml/7 fl oz water and the vinegar to the boil in a pan. Add the chillies, shallots, ginger, sugar and mustard seeds. Then add the marrow and chopped dill, season with salt and pepper and simmer everything for about 3 minutes. Allow the mixture to cool and let stand for about 2 hours.

4 The chutney will keep in well-sealed jars for up to 3 weeks in the refrigerator.

GREEN TOMATO CHUTNEY

Makes 7–8 230 ml/8 fl oz jars

1.5 kg/3¼ lb green tomatoes
500 g/1 lb 2 oz onions
½ tsp salt
100 g/3½ oz dried dates
500 ml/18 fl oz vinegar
300 g/10½ oz sugar
1 Tbsp mustard
½ Tbsp curry powder
½ Tbsp cayenne pepper
½ Tbsp ground curcuma
½ Tbsp ground ginger
Mild paprika powder

1 Wash the tomatoes, peel the onion and roughly chop both. Salt them, cover and leave to stand overnight. The following day, drain off the liquid. Stone and finely cube the dates. Mix them with the vinegar, sugar and tomato and onion mixture, and bring to the boil.

2 Simmer without a lid for an hour, stirring occasionally. Add the mustard and the spices after 45 minutes. Boil over a high heat for a further 5 to 7 minutes to thicken. Immediately fill twist-off-lid jars with the mixture, seal tightly and stand upside down for 5 minutes.

There is no better recipe for unripe tomatoes at the end of the summer than that for green tomato chutney. It is simple to make and tastes delicious with pan-fried meat.

PUMPKIN AND TOMATO CHUTNEY

Makes 6 230 ml/8 fl oz jars

4–6 tomatoes (about 600 g/1 lb 5 oz)
800 g/1³/₄ lb pumpkin flesh
4 onions
4 cloves garlic
Vegetable oil
2 Tbsp mustard powder
2 tsp crushed peppercorns
1–2 sticks cinnamon
Salt
200 g/7 oz sugar
4–5 Tbsp vinegar

1 Scald the tomatoes with boiling water, skin them and remove the stalk-eyes. Remove the seeds and cut the tomatoes into cubes.

2 Cut the pumpkin into cubes. Peel and chop the onions and garlic.

3 Heat a little oil in a pan. Sweat the chopped garlic and onion in the oil for 2 to 3 minutes until glassy. Then add the remaining ingredients and stew together, stirring continuously. Bring the vegetable mixture to the boil, then cook over a low heat for about 30 minutes until a thick chutney is achieved.

4 Fill rinsed jars with the hot mixture and seal well. The chutney will keep for between 3 and 4 months when stored in a cool place. It tastes wonderful served with both meat and fish.

RED CURRY PASTE

Makes 1 230 ml/8 fl oz jar

8 red pepperonis
1/2 bunch spring onions
1 stem lemon grass
6 cloves garlic
1 2 cm/3/4 in piece galgant root
1 kaffir lime
3 Tbsp sesame oil
1/2 tsp ground cumin
Salt
1/2 tsp freshly grated nutmeg
Pepper
1 tsp shrimp paste

1 Wash the pepperonis, cut lengthways, remove the seeds and cut into strips. Clean, wash and finely chop the spring onions and the lemon grass. Peel and finely chop the garlic. Peel the galgant root and cut into pieces. Rinse the kaffir lime in lukewarm water, peel it and finely chop the rind.

2 Heat the oil in a pan and sweat the pepperonis, spring onions, lemon grass, garlic, galgant and lime peel in it. Season with the ground cumin, salt, nutmeg and pepper.

3 Tip the mixture into a bowl and crush with a pestle to a creamy paste. Finally, mix in the shrimp paste. The curry paste will keep cooled in a well-sealed container for 2 months.

Tip
Red curry paste is a well-known and much used ingredient in Thai cuisine. It lends an arousing heat to crunchy-cooked vegetables from the wok.

FRUIT CHUTNEYS

RHUBARB CHUTNEY

Makes 4 500 ml/18 fl oz jars

500 g/1 lb 2 oz rhubarb
200 g/7 oz strawberries
400 g/14 oz onions
800 g/1¾ lb brown sugar
500 ml/18 fl oz white wine vinegar
1 tsp salt
1 tsp ground coriander
¼ tsp ground cloves

1 Wash the fruit. Cut the rhubarb into pieces; top the strawberries and cut into quarters. Peel the onions and cut into small cubes. Put everything into a pan together with the sugar, vinegar and spices and bring to the boil.

2 Cook for 1 to 2 hours over medium heat, stirring regularly.

3 Fill the jars with the hot chutney and seal immediately.

ROWANBERRY CHUTNEY

Makes 5 500 ml/ 18 fl oz jars

700 g/1 lb 9 oz rowanberries
300 g/10½ oz onions
200 g/7 oz tomatoes
2 red peppers
400 ml/14 fl oz red wine vinegar
2 Tbsp sultanas
1 tsp salt
1 tsp pepper
¼ tsp cinnamon
1 large pinch cayenne pepper
500 g/1 lb 2 oz jam sugar

1 Remove the washed rowanberries from their stalks and place in the deep freezer for 24 hours (this makes them less bitter). Then pour a vinegar and water solution (half vinegar and half water) over the berries and leave to stand overnight.

2 The next day, drain the berries with a sieve. Cut the peeled onions into small cubes. Skin the tomatoes and cut into small pieces. Remove the seeds from the red peppers and cut into cubes. Put all these ingredients, together with the rowanberries, red wine vinegar, sultanas and spices into a pan and bring to the boil.

3 Cook for an hour over a medium heat. Stir in the jam sugar and bring to the boil again, stirring all the time. Boil for 4 minutes, then fill the jars with the hot mixture and seal immediately.

OLIVE PASTE

Serves 4

200 g/7 oz black olives (from the jar)
4 cloves garlic
1 bunch parsley
4 Tbsp olive oil
Freshly ground pepper
2 Tbsp garlic oil

1 Drain the olives. Peel and press the garlic.

2 Wash the parsley, shake dry and finely chop.

3 Using a hand blender, mix the parsley, olives, garlic and oil to a puree, then season well with salt and pepper. The paste will keep well chilled and in a sealed container for about 2 months.

TOMATO CHUTNEY

Makes 4 250 ml/9 fl oz jars

750 g/1³/₄ lb tomatoes
500 g/1 lb 2 oz onions
250 g/9 oz cooking apples
200 ml/7 fl oz white wine vinegar
250 g/9 oz crystallised brown sugar
1 level Tbsp salt
2 Tbsp mild paprika powder
¹/₂ tsp chilli powder
1 large pinch each: ground cloves
            and ground allspice

1 Cut a cross in the tomato skins, scald with boiling water, remove the skins and quarter. Peel the onions and cut into cubes. Peel the apples and coarsely grate.

2 Place the prepared ingredients and the vinegar in a pan and bring to the boil, stirring all the time. Add the sugar and salt. Cook the complete mixture over a medium heat for about 40 minutes, stirring occasionally, then season with the spices.

3 Rinse the jars in hot water and fill with the chutney, which is delicious with pan-fried meat or with fresh ciabatta or focaccia.

Tip
A pretty jar filled with this tomato chutney makes an excellent gift for a friend.

SPICY KETCHUP

Makes 3 500 ml/18 fl oz jars

500 g/1 lb 2 oz red peppers
500 g/1 lb 2 oz green peppers
4 red pepperonis
700 g/1 lb 9 oz red onions
4 cloves garlic
6 Tbsp sesame oil
3 allspice berries
2 juniper berries
3 cloves
1 large pinch cumin
Hot paprika powder according to taste
250 ml/9 fl oz meat stock
4 Tbsp red wine vinegar

1 Wash, dry and halve the peppers. Remove the seeds, the cut the peppers into small pieces. Wash, dry and halve the pepperonis. Remove the seeds and finely chop the pepperonis. Peel the onions and cut them into cubes.

2 Peel and finely chop the garlic. Heat the oil in a pan and sweat the onions, peppers, pepperoni and garlic.

3 Season the vegetables with the spices and pour in the stock and vinegar. Cover and simmer over a medium heat for about an hour. Finally, pass the mixture through a fine sieve and season once again with the spices.

CHERRY CHUTNEY

Makes 1 230 ml/8 fl oz jar

1 cooking apple
1 red onion
1 small jar sour cherries (370 ml/13 fl oz)
20 ml/4 tsp red wine vinegar
$^1/_2$ Tbsp mustard seeds
$^1/_2$ Tbsp coriander seeds
$^1/_4$ tsp chopped ginger
Several chopped rosemary leaves
Salt
Freshly ground pepper
Sugar according to taste

1 Peel the apple, cut into quarters and remove the core. Peel the onions and, together with the apple, cut up into small cubes.

2 Bring to the boil the cherries with their juice, together with the apple, onions, vinegar, mustard seeds, coriander seeds, ginger and rosemary, then simmer without a lid for about 30 minutes. Season the chutney with salt, pepper and sugar according to taste.

3 Fill the prepared jar with the mixture while still hot, seal immediately and leave to cool. This chutney goes especially well with camembert.

COURGETTE AND ONION RELISH

Tip

The chillies lose a lot of their heat when the seeds are removed.

Those who prefer their food especially fiery can leave the seeds in.

Makes 6 250 ml/9 fl oz jars

1 kg/2¼ lb courgettes
1 kg/2¼ lb onions
125 ml/4½ fl oz rapeseed oil
3 red chillies
3 cloves garlic
125 ml/4½ fl oz dry sherry
100 ml/3½ fl oz white wine vinegar
Salt
Pepper
3 Tbsp sugar

1 Trim and wash the courgettes. Peel the onions. Finely chop both.

2 Sweat the finely chopped courgettes and onions in the rapeseed oil for about 10 minutes over medium heat.

3 In the meantime, clean and wash the chillies, remove the seeds and cut the chillies into fine rings. Peel the garlic and finely chop it. Combine the chillies and garlic together with the sherry, vinegar, salt, pepper and the sugar. Add the mixture to the vegetables and sweat for a further 20 minutes. Fill the jars with the mixture and seal tightly.

MEDITERRANEAN RELISH

Makes 2–3 500 ml/18 fl oz jars

1 small yellow and 1 small green pepper
1 small aubergine
400 g/14 oz courgettes
3 red onions
2 cloves garlic
1 Tbsp vegetable oil
125 ml/4½ fl oz white wine
150 ml/¼ pint vegetable stock
100 ml/3½ fl oz tomato juice
6 Tbsp cider vinegar
2 Tbsp tomato puree
¼ tsp black pepper
¼ tsp cayenne pepper
Salt
3 tsp crushed thyme
1–2 tsp mixed Italian herbs
120 g/4½ oz brown sugar

1 Halve the peppers and, together with the other vegetables, clean, wash and chop into fine cubes. Peel both the onions and the garlic. Chop the onions into fine cubes and crush the garlic. Sweat both in the heated oil, then add the cubed vegetables.

2 Deglaze with the white wine, vegetable stock, tomato juice and vinegar, then add the tomato puree. Season the relish well with the herbs and spices, then simmer for about 10 minutes, stirring all the time.

3 Add the sugar and cook the relish for a further 10 minutes. Then, as with jam, fill the prepared preserving jars with the mixture while it is still hot. Seal the jars and boil as desired.

TWO ITALIAN SAUCES FOR PASTA

TOMATO SAUCE

Makes 2 500 ml/18 fl oz jars

1 kg/2¼ lb tomatoes
1 clove garlic
1 medium-sized onion
2 small carrots (80 g/2¾ oz)
1 stalk celery
Several basil leaves
5 Tbsp olive oil
Sea salt
Freshly ground white pepper

1 Slit a cross in the tomato skins, scald with boiling water, remove the skins and cut the tomatoes into pieces. Remove the seeds. Peel the garlic and onion, leave the garlic whole but cut the onion into cubes. Trim the carrots and celery, wash and cut up into small pieces.

2 Heat the olive oil, briefly fry the garlic in it, then remove and dispose of the clove. Add the onion and vegetable pieces and fry briefly in the oil. Add the tomato pieces.

3 Simmer with a lid over a low heat for about 30 minutes, stirring occasionally. Cut the basil leaves into strips. Add to the tomato and vegetable mixture 5 minutes before the end of the cooking time and season with salt and pepper. Finally, pass the mixture through a sieve.

4 Fill the jars with the cooled sauce and store in the refrigerator.

BASIL SAUCE (PESTO)

Makes 1 230 ml/8 fl oz jar

10 cloves garlic
200 g/7 oz pine kernels
2–3 bunches fresh basil
        (about 40–50 leaves)
1 tsp coarse sea salt
3 Tbsp small pecorino cubes
3 Tbsp parmesan cheese
250 ml/9 fl oz virgin olive oil

1 Peel the garlic, finely chop it together with the pine kernels, and crush with a pestle and mortar. Only dab dry the basil leaves, then cut into strips and grind it with the salt in the mortar. Remove and put to one side.

2 Combine the olive oil with the other ingredients until they form a smooth paste. Pesto can also be made in a kitchen mixer, though you should take care that the ingredients are not ground too finely.

HERBAL OILS &
SEASONED VINEGARS

HERBAL VINEGAR VARIATIONS

Tip
Make sure the fresh herbs you use are perfectly clean and dry. Any impurities will make the vinegar cloudy.

BASIL VINEGAR

Makes about 1 litre/1³/₄ pints

2–3 sprigs fresh basil
2 cloves garlic
1 l/1³/₄ pints wine vinegar
(red or white wine vinegar)

1 Wash and dab dry the herbs. Peel the garlic. Place both in a bottle and pour over the vinegar. Let stand for at least 14 days.

2 Occasionally swing the bottle slightly from side to side. Pass the vinegar through a fine cloth and into a second bottle. Store in a cool and dark place.

GARLIC VINEGAR

Makes about 500 ml/18 fl oz

100 ml/3¹/₂ fl oz vinegar essence (25%)
100 ml/3¹/₂ fl oz water
300 ml/10¹/₂ fl oz rosé wine
6 medium-sized peeled cloves garlic

1 Mix together the vinegar essence, water and rosé wine and pour into a bottle or carafe.

2 Add the garlic, seal the container and leave to stand for 5 to 6 days. Afterwards, filter into a second container and seal.

Provencal Herbal Vinegar

Makes about 500 ml/18 fl oz

100 ml/3$^1/_2$ fl oz vinegar essence (25%)
100 ml/3$^1/_2$ fl oz water
300 ml/10$^1/_2$ fl oz white wine
1 bunch fresh Provencal mixed herbs
      (basil, rosemary, thyme,
      tarragon)

1 Rinse the herbs, spin them in a cloth until dry, then put into a wide-necked bottle. Mix together the vinegar essence, water and wine, pour over the herbs and then seal the bottle.

2 Leave to stand for 10 days, then filter into a second bottle and seal.

The vinegar keeps its light colour when stored in a dark, cool place.

115

AROMATIC VINEGARS

ROSE VINEGAR

Makes about 500 ml/18 fl oz

40 g/1¹/₂ oz dried red rose petals
500 ml/18 fl oz white wine vinegar

1 Sort the rose petals, rinse and dab dry. Pour the vinegar into a jar with a lid and add the petals.

2 Leave the sealed jar containing the rose vinegar to stand in a warm place for 10 days. Shake a little each day. Then filter through a fine cloth into a bottle. Store in a dark place.

HERBAL VINEGAR

Makes about 500 ml/18 fl oz

Herbs according to taste (e.g. thyme, sage, tarragon, dill, basil)
500 ml/18 fl oz white wine vinegar

1 Wash the herbs carefully, shake them dry and put into a sealable jar or glass bottle.

2 Top up with the vinegar, seal the jar or bottle well and leave to stand for 14 days. Finally, filter through a fine muslin cloth.

RASPBERRY VINEGAR

Makes about 500 ml/18 fl oz

500 ml/18 fl oz white wine vinegar
15 raspberries
40 g/1¹/₂ oz tarragon leaves

1 Sort the berries, wash and dab dry. Put them in a wide-necked jar together with the tarragon leaves. Fill up with the vinegar and seal well.

2 Leave the vinegar to stand on a sunny windowsill for 14 days. Then, filter through a fine muslin cloth and pour into a bottle. Store in a dark place.

Tip
Raspberry vinegar tastes delicious with fish, fruit salad, or in an asparagus vinaigrette.

SPICY TEQUILA VINEGAR

Makes 500 ml/18 fl oz

2 sprigs rosemary
2 small chillies
10 white peppercorns
200 ml/ 7 fl oz tequila
100 ml/3$^1/_2$ fl oz vinegar essence

1 Wash and dry the rosemary and pluck off the individual needles. Wash the chillies. Put the peppercorns into a clean, decorative bottle toge- ther with the rosemary needles and the chillies.

2 Mix together the tequila, vinegar and 200 ml/7 fl oz of water and also add to the bottle.

3 Seal the bottle and leave to stand for about 5 days, then pour through a filter. The vinegar is then ready to be processed further accord- ing to taste.

HERBAL OIL

Makes 500 ml/18 fl oz

10 g/¹⁄₃ oz flaked hazelnuts
1 sprig each: thyme, sage and marjoram
500 ml/18 fl oz olive oil

1 Dry roast the nuts in a pan. Remove them and set aside to cool.

2 Wash the herbs, shake dry and put them into a bottle together with the nuts. Add the oil and seal the bottle tightly.

3 Leave the herbal oil to stand for about 14 days. Finally, filter it through a fine muslin cloth. Stored in a cool and dark place, the oil will keep for about 6 weeks.

ROSEMARY OIL

Makes 500 ml/18 fl oz

1–2 sprigs fresh rosemary
500 ml/18 fl oz rapeseed oil

1 Wash the rosemary, shake it dry and put into a bottle. Pour on the oil, seal the bottle and leave to stand for 14 days, then remove the sprigs of rosemary. Leaving the rosemary in the bottle gives it a more decorative appearance. If so desired, only small amounts of the oil should be made for immediate use, otherwise the oil may become bitter.

Tip
Herbal oils are ideal for frying chops and steaks, as well as for use in salads.

GRANDMOTHER'S TRADITIONAL SEASONED VINEGARS

GARLIC AND RED WINE VINEGAR

Makes 750 ml/1 pint 7 fl oz

1 sprig each basil, tarragon and
      lemon balm
6 cloves garlic
1 bay leaf
1 Tbsp coarsely ground black
      peppercorns
100 ml/3½ fl oz vinegar essence (25%)
500 ml/18 fl oz strong red wine

1 Wash the herbs, shake dry and leave for 1 to 2 days to dry thoroughly.

2 Peel the garlic and cut it in half. Together with the herbs, put into a wide-necked bottle. Add the bay leaf, pepper, vinegar essence and red wine.

3 Seal the bottle and leave to stand for about 3 weeks. Then, pass through a sieve and pour into bottles. Seal and store airtight.

JUNIPER VINEGAR

Makes 1 litre/1¾ pints

1 bunch burnet herb
2 sprigs tarragon
2 Tbsp juniper berries
1 l/1¾ pints white wine vinegar

1 Sort the herbs, unwashed, and place them into a bottle together with the juniper berries and the white wine vinegar. Seal the bottle tightly.

2 Leave the vinegar to stand for at least 4 weeks. Then filter through a fine muslin cloth, once again pour into a bottle and seal tightly. Juniper vinegar is suitable for seasoning sauces for game, fine butter sauces and sauce béarnaise, as well as for salads with red meat or marinating meat before frying or grilling.

Herbs

Dill, thyme and sage are Mediterranean herbs that have long become a part of our culinary lives and that can be grown well in every sunny garden or balcony.

Fine-leafed dill possesses a refreshingly tangy aroma. All parts of the plant that grow above ground can be used. Dill is traditionally used to season salads and fish dishes.

Thyme is rich in essential oils that give the herb its tangy taste and aroma. Thyme is usually used to season sauces together with marjoram.

Sage is a herb used both medicinally and for seasoning food. It has a strong fresh and slightly bitter taste and a balmy aroma. It can be recognised by its felt-like silver-green leaves.

DILL VINEGAR

Makes about 500 ml/18 fl oz

100 ml/3¹/₂ fl oz vinegar essence (25%)
100 ml/ 3¹/₂ fl oz water
300 ml/10¹/₂ fl oz white wine
6–8 sprigs dill

1 Mix together the vinegar essence, water and white wine in a bowl and pour into a bottle containing the dill.

2 Seal the bottle and leave to stand for 4 to 5 days. Then filter into a second bottle and seal.

THYME VINEGAR

Makes about 500 ml/18 fl oz

100 ml/3¹/₂ fl oz vinegar essence (25%)
100 ml/3¹/₂ fl oz water
300 ml/10¹/₂ fl oz white wine
6–8 sprigs thyme

1 Mix together the vinegar essence, water and white wine in a bowl and pour into a bottle containing the thyme.

2 Seal the bottle and leave to stand for 4 to 5 days, turning it occasionally. Then filter into a second bottle and seal.

SAGE VINEGAR

Makes 500 ml/18 fl oz

100 ml/3$\frac{1}{2}$ fl oz vinegar essence (25%)
100 ml/3$\frac{1}{2}$ fl oz water
300 ml/10$\frac{1}{2}$ fl oz rosé wine
4–6 sprigs sage

1 Mix together the vinegar essence, water and rosé wine in a bowl and pour into a bottle containing the sage.

2 Seal the bottle and leave to stand for 4 to 5 days, turning it occasionally. Then filter into a second bottle and seal.

ORANGE VINEGAR

Makes 500 ml/18 fl oz

100 ml/3$\frac{1}{2}$ fl oz vinegar essence (25%)
100 ml/3$\frac{1}{2}$ fl oz water
300 ml/10$\frac{1}{2}$ fl oz white wine
1 Tbsp orange juice
Peel of 1 untreated orange

1 Mix together the vinegar essence, water, wine and orange juice and pour into a bottle. Thinly peel the orange rind and remove the pith.

2 Add the peel to the bottle, seal the bottle and leave to stand for 4 to 5 days. Then filter it into a second bottle and seal.

LIQUEURS, JUICES & SCHNAPPS

Nut Liqueur

Tip

Try serving the nut liqueur topped with whipped cream for a change. It gives the liqueur a creamier taste.

Makes 1 700 ml/1¼ pint bottle

100 g/3½ oz shelled walnuts
100 g/3½ oz crystallised sugar
500 ml/18 fl oz brandy

1 The nuts should be fresh from the tree to ensure the shells can be removed easily. Mix the nut halves together with the sugar and brandy and leave to stand in a coloured glass bottle in a warm place for 6 weeks. Then filter and bottle.

ELDERBERRY LIQUEUR

Makes 7 700 ml/1 ¼ pint bottles

2.5 l/about 4½ pints elderberry juice
1.5 kg/3 lb 5 oz sugar
1 vanilla pod
1 cinnamon stick
6 Tbsp lemon juice
500 ml/18 fl oz rum (54% alc. vol.)

1 Cut the vanilla pod in pieces.
Bring the elderberry juice to the
boil with the sugar, vanilla and cinnamon. Add the lemon juice.

2 Pour the liquor into a large container and leave to cool. Then add
the rum, filter the mixture through a
fine muslin cloth and fill bottles with
the liqueur. Seal the bottles tightly.

You can also make the elderberry
juice yourself. The recipe can be
found on page 136.

CREME DE COCO

1 coconut (about 200 g/
            7 oz coconut flesh)
120 g/4¼ oz white crystallised sugar
1 Tbsp vanilla sugar
250 ml/9 fl oz white rum (54 % alc. vol.)
4 Tbsp dried banana chips

1 Using a strong corkscrew, bore a hole in one of the coconut's eyes. Allow the coconut milk to drain away, then smash the nut with a hammer, remove the flesh and cut into pieces. Put into a container together with the crystallised sugar.

2 Add the vanilla sugar, rum and banana chips. Seal the container with a twist-on lid or clamps. Leave to stand for about 3 to 4 weeks.

EGGNOG

(Illustration opposite)
Makes 1 500 ml/18 fl oz bottle

4 egg yolks
200 g/7 oz sugar
½ vanilla pod
250 ml/9 fl oz milk
100 ml/3¼ fl oz pure alcohol
            (from a chemist)

1 Beat the egg yolks and sugar until foamy. Slice open the vanilla pod lengthways and scrape out the mark.

2 Add the vanilla mark, milk and alcohol to the egg and sugar. Mix together well and leave to stand in a cool place.

3 The eggnog can be drunk after 24 hours. In sealed bottles, the liqueur will keep for about 4 weeks in the refrigerator.

ROSEHIP LIQUEUR

Makes 2 700 ml/1¼ pint bottles

500 g/1 lb 2 oz rosehips
500 ml/18 fl oz wine alcohol (chemist)
500 ml/18 fl oz korn schnapps
1 kg/2¼ lb sugar

1 Remove the stalks from the rose-hips, which should be picked after the first frost, then either crush them in a pot or chop finely with a mixer.

2 Pour the alcohol and the schnapps over the rosehips.

3 Boil the sugar in 750 ml/1 pint 7 fl oz water for about 15 minutes until it becomes a syrup. Pour this over the fruit while still hot. Fill a large jar with the liquor, seal tightly and leave to stand for about 14 days on a sunny windowsill.

4 After 14 days, pass the liquor through a linen cloth several times, then bottle. Leave to stand for about 4 weeks before drinking.

LEMON LIQUEUR

Makes 1 700 ml/1¼ pint bottle

2 untreated lemons
500 ml/18 fl oz vodka
100 g/3½ oz sugar

1 Rinse the lemons under hot water and very thinly peel the rind. Then squeeze the juice.

2 Mix the lemon peel, juice and vodka with 1 litre/1¾ pints water and pour into a large sealable bottle.

3 Combine the sugar with 125 ml/ 4½ fl oz water and boil for several minutes. Allow to cool slightly and then add to the vodka mixture. Shake well, then leave to stand, tightly sealed, for 24 hours in the refrigerator.

4 Finally, pass the bottle's content through a sieve lined with a muslin cloth, pour into a bottle rinsed with boiling water and seal tightly.

JUNIPER APERITIF

Makes 1 700 ml/1¼ pint bottle

30 g/1 oz fresh juniper berries
3–4 small sprigs juniper
700 ml/1¼ pints dry white wine
5 Tbsp sugar

1 Sort the berries, wash them and dry well. Put all the ingredients into a large bottle and seal tightly.

2 Leave the aperitif to stand for 1 week, then pour through a fine muslin cloth and fill bottles with the filtered liqueur. Seal the bottles well.

WALNUT LIQUEUR

Makes 2 700 ml/1¼ pint bottles

25 g/1 oz green, unripe walnuts
1 l/1¾ pints brandy
½ tsp ground cinnamon
500 g/1 lb 2 oz sugar

1 Crush the walnuts and put them in a bottle with the brandy and cinnamon. Seal the bottle and leave to stand for 3 weeks in a sunny place. Then filter through a fine muslin cloth.

2 Boil the sugar in about 1 litre/ 1¾ pints of water until the sugar is dissolved. Allow the sugar solution to cool, then mix together with the brandy. Fill the mixture into a large bottle and seal tightly.

3 Leave the bottle to stand for 2 to 3 days, sieve the contents again and pour into clean bottles.

ROSE LIQUEUR

**Makes 1 750 ml/
1 pint 7 fl oz bottle**

**75 g/2½ oz petals from scented roses
250 ml/9 fl oz vodka
375 g/13 oz sugar**

1 Carefully sort the rose petals, discarding damaged ones. Wash and dry them and put into a bottle. Pour the vodka over the petals.

2 Seal the bottle and leave to stand in a dark place for 14 days at room temperature. Then boil the sugar and 500 ml/18 fl oz water to a syrup and allow to cool.

3 Mix the rose vodka and the sugar solution together and pour into a bottle through a linen cloth. Store for several weeks before enjoying the liqueur.

PINE NEEDLE BITTERS

Makes 1 litre/1³/₄ pint bottle

150 g/5 oz young pine needles
700 ml/1¹/₄ pints alcohol (korn,
      schnapps or pure alcohol)
2 Tbsp sugar

1 Put the pine needles into a wide-necked bottle and pour on enough alcohol to cover well. Let stand for about a week until the liquid becomes light yellow. Then pour through a muslin cloth. Stirring continuously, dissolve the sugar in the liquor and and pour it into a clean bottle. Seal the bottle well.

CINNAMON LIQUEUR

Makes 1 litre/1¾ pint bottle

½ orange
6–8 cinnamon sticks
125 g/4½ oz brown or crystallised sugar
1 bottle of brandy (700 ml/1¼ pints)

1 Squeeze the juice from the half orange. Add the cinnamon and brown sugar to the juice, and put the whole mixture into a bottle. Pour in the brandy, seal the bottle and leave to stand for about 4 weeks. Then filter through a sieve lined with a muslin cloth and fill a decorative bottle (holding at least 800 ml/1 pint 8 fl oz) with the liqueur.

Cinnamon

Cinnamon is one of the spices obtained from tree bark. Three main sorts are cultivated: Ceylon cinnamon, Chinese cinnamon and Padang cinnamon. Cinnamon has been in use for a very long time. Both the ancient Egyptians and the Romans used it as a medicine and as a cosmetic.

Cinnamon's origins can be traced back to Sri Lanka, which was conquered by the Portuguese during the 16th century in part because of this spice.

Cinnamon trees are cultivated in cinnamon gardens. The tender branches are pruned from the fast growing trees. The finest bark is to be found on the thin shoots in the middle of the plant. The bark is freed from a cork covering, rolled by hand and dried in the shade. The so-called "quills" are then cut into uniform sticks of about 10 cm/4 in in length.

ELDERBERRY JUICE

Makes 2 700 ml/1 ¼ pint bottles

**1 kg/2¼ lb elderberries
     with stalks removed
250 g/9 oz sugar
1 large pinch ground cinnamon**

1 Wash the elderberries, dab dry, remove the stalks and pass the fruit through a sieve.

2 Boil the resulting juice together with the sugar and cinnamon for several minutes, skimming the foam often.

3 Fill the bottles with the hot juice and seal them immediately. The syrupy juice may be diluted with water according to taste. Elderberry juice is a tried and true household remedy for colds. A steam juicer is recommended for making larger quantities.

BLACKBERRY SYRUP

**Makes 2 750 ml/
1 pint 7 fl oz bottles**

2 kg/4½ lb blackberries
About 2 kg/4½ lb sugar
  (according to quantity of juice)
120 ml/4½ fl oz lemon juice

1 Wash the blackberries under flowing water and drain well. Put the berries either through a juicer or through a fine sieve. In addition, pass the berries through a mincer on the finest setting, then pass the pulp through a sieve. Leave the juice to stand in a large jar or jug in a dark place at room temperature for 2 days.

2 Remove the skin from the juice and filter the liquid through a fine muslin cloth. Measure out the resulting juice. Per litre/1¾ pints juice, bring to the boil 1.5 kg/3 lb 5 oz sugar, 200 ml/7 fl oz of water and 60 ml/ 2 fl oz lemon juice, stirring continuously. Add the blackberry juice and simmer over a low heat for 2 to 3 minutes.

3 Skim off the resulting foam often, stir well and reduce to a syrup. Fill the bottles with the finished syrup and seal well immediately.

MEAT
& FISH

HOMEMADE SPECIALITIES

BLACK PUDDING

Makes 6 500 g/1 lb 2 oz jars

500 g/1 lb 2 oz fresh pork rind
50 g/1³/₄ oz salt
1 kg/2¹/₄ lb neck of pork
500 g/1 lb 2 oz belly pork
1 onion
20 g/³/₄ oz margarine
750 ml/1 pint 7 fl oz pig's blood
250 ml/9 fl oz pork stock
4–6 pinches dried marjoram
4–5 pinches ground cloves
3–4 pinches pepper
3–4 pinches paté seasoning

Tip
Fresh pig's blood must be ordered in advance from your butcher.

1 Soak the pork rind in water for 1 to 2 hours, changing the water in between. Put in a pot, cover with fresh cold water and bring to the boil. Skim, then add half the salt, the neck of pork and the belly pork.

2 Peel the onion, cut into halves or quarters, briefly fry in hot butter while stirring, then add to the meat.

3 Cover the pot and simmer for 1 to 1¹/₂ hours. Remove the rind as soon as it is soft, pass half through the mincer twice and immediately stir into the blood to prevent clumping.

4 Cut the other half and the belly pork into small pieces as desired, mix together with the cooked, finely cubed neck of pork and leave to stand for 15 minutes.

5 Stir the meat mixture into the blood, add the remaining salt, the spices and the stock, and mix well. Allow the mixture to cool thoroughly for about 10 minutes before filling clean preserving jars.

6 Fill the jars up to about 4 cm/ 1¹/₂ in from the rim and seal immediately with rubber rings, glass lids and clamps. Put them into a preserving pan filled with cold water and cook for 120 minutes at 100 °C/212 °F.

FINE SAGE AND LIVER TIMBALE

Serves 4

500 g/1 lb 2 oz spinach
Salt
400 g/14 oz calf's liver
100 g/3½ oz fresh fat bacon
2 Tbsp brandy
125 ml/4½ fl oz white wine
Pepper
6 sage leaves
2 eggs, whisked
100 g/3½ oz white breadcrumbs
Cumberland sauce as an accompaniment

1 Clean the spinach and blanch in boiling salted water for about 2 minutes. Plunge into cold water and drain well.

2 Clean the calf's liver and, together with the fat bacon, cut into coarse cubes.

3 Mix together the brandy, wine, salt and pepper. Stir into the meat and leave to marinate for about 30 minutes.

4 Wash the sage, shake dry and finely chop.

5 Remove the meat from the marinade and pass through the mincer. Stir the sage, eggs and breadcrumbs into the mixture.

6 Line 4 timbale forms with the spinach leaves. Fill with the liver mixture and cover with spinach leaves.

7 Cook the timbales in a water bath for about 30 minutes. Remove, turn upside down onto a plate to free the mixture from the form, garnish and serve with Cumberland sauce.

Liver Paté with Walnuts

Serves 4

250 g/9 oz chicken livers
5 sage leaves
1 tsp oil
1 tsp soya sauce
Salt
Freshly ground black pepper
Worcestershire sauce
100 g/3½ oz butter
10 walnuts

1 Wash, dry and cut the liver into cubes. Together with the sage, fry the cubes in oil for about 3 minutes.

Reduce the heat and leave to stand for about 5 minutes; the liver should still be pink inside.

2 Puree half the lukewarm liver together with the sage, seasonings and butter, then season to taste with salt and pepper. Cut the rest of the liver into strips and quarter the walnuts.

3 Layer the liver puree, liver strips and nuts in a suitable form and chill. To serve, turn upside down onto a plate to free the paté from the form and cut into slices.

143

CONFIT DE CANARD

Sufficient for a 2 litre/
3½ pint ceramic form

1 duck e.g. Barbarie duck
    (about 1.8 kg/4 lb)
2 tsp black peppercorns
4 bay leaves
2 cloves
250 g/9 oz coarse sea salt
2 cloves garlic
2–3 sprigs thyme
2 onions
A little olive oil for frying
500 ml/18 fl oz red wine
Grated peel of ½ an untreated lemon
1 pinch cardamom

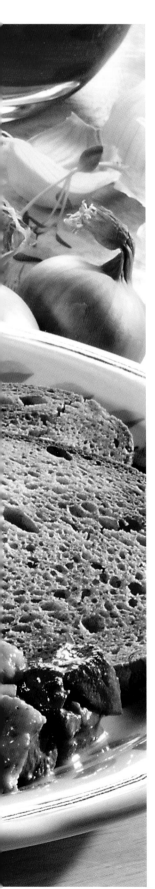

1 Halve the duck lengthways. Cut the halves in two just before the duck thighs and remove the leaf fat. Wash the duck pieces and fat, dry, and chill the fat. Grind the peppercorns, bay leaves and cloves in a mortar and mix with the salt. Peel the garlic.

2 Wash and shake dry the thyme. Lay the meat, garlic and thyme into a ceramic bowl. Spread the seasoned salt over the meat, cover and leave to stand in the refrigerator for a day.

3 The next day, rub the salt from the meat. Bone the duck and cut into cubes. Peel the onions and cut into fine cubes. Roast the meat and onions in a pan with a little olive oil. Pour in the red wine and add the lemon peel and the cardamom.

4 Cook everything for about 20 to 35 minutes, until tender. Season the tenderly cooked meat with salt and turn the contents of the pan into a terrine form.

5 Prick the surface many times with a long fork to allow the fat to come to the surface. Heat the leaf fat and slowly pour over the meat. The confit must be carefully covered with a layer of fat to preserve the meat.

6 Covered, the confit will keep in the refrigerator for several weeks. Alternatively, the confit may be preserved in jars. Fill clean jars with the mixture, seal the jars airtight and sterilise in a water bath for 30 minutes. Remove the jars and allow to cool slowly.

145

SQUIRE'S TERRINE

Serves 4–6

750 g/1 lb 11 oz mixed minced meat
100 g/3¹/₂ oz breadcrumbs
2 eggs
1 bunch parsley
2 cloves garlic
2 chillies
3 Tbsp olive oil
1 tin peeled tomatoes (380 g/13¹/₂ oz)
175 g/6 oz fresh fat bacon
Salt
Pepper
1 tsp dried thyme
Cumberland sauce as an accompaniment

1 Knead the minced meat, bread-crumbs and eggs to a dough. Wash the parsley, shake dry, chop finely and add to the meat mixture.

2 Peel the garlic and chop it finely. Clean the chillies and dice them finely. Heat the oil and briefly fry the garlic and chillies in it. Add the tomatoes and cook, uncovered, for about 10 minutes. Finally blend to a puree in a mixer.

3 Cut the fat bacon into slices and use them to line a suitable terrine form. Mix together the minced meat and vegetable puree, season with salt, pepper and thyme, and fill the terrine form with the mixture.

4 Cover the form with a lid and cook in a water bath for about 1¹/₂ hours. Remove and allow to cool. Cut the terrine into slices and serve with the Cumberland sauce.

RILLETTES DE LAPIN

Serves 4–6

80 g/2³/₄ oz stoned dried prunes
3 Tbsp brandy
1.2 kg/2 lb 10 oz boned rabbit
1 rabbit's liver
Freshly ground black pepper
Salt
Grated peel of 1 untreated lemon
75 g/2¹/₂ oz smoked streaky bacon
3 sprigs thyme, chopped
3 sprigs rosemary, chopped
1 bay leaf
500 ml/18 fl oz white wine
500 ml/ 18 fl oz game stock
75 ml/2¹/₂ fl oz extra virgin olive oil

1 Cut the prunes into small pieces, add the brandy and put to one side. Cut the rabbit into rough cubes. Wash and dry the liver. Season both kinds of meat with salt and pepper and rub with the lemon peel, then put into a bowl. Cut the streaky bacon into cubes.

2 Add the herbs, streaky bacon, prunes in brandy and bay leaf to the meat. Pour the white wine, game stock and olive oil over the meat mixture. Cover and leave to stand in the refrigerator overnight.

3 The next day, preheat the oven to 180 °C/355 °F/gas mark 4. Firmly layer half the meat mixture in a terrine form. Cut the marinated liver into slices and place on the meat. Layer the rest of the meat on top of the liver. Seal the terrine lid well. Bake the rillettes in a water bath in the oven at 180 °C/ 355 °F/gas mark 4 for 1¹/₂ hours. Allow to cool, then chill for 24 hours.

THREE GOURMET TERRINES

OLD ENGLISH HUNTING TERRINE

Serves 4–6

150 g/5 oz shallots
1 Tbsp butter
1 bunch marjoram
200 g/7 oz shoulder of pork
250 g/9 oz venison
Salt and pepper
Seasoning for game
1 Tbsp port wine
2 eggs
2 Tbsp pistachio nuts
100 g streaky bacon
Cumberland sauce

1 Peel and finely chop the shallots. Heat the butter and sweat the chopped shallots in it for 5 minutes.

Finely chop the marjoram. Pass the pork and the venison through the mincer on the finest setting and knead the shallots and marjoram into the mixture. Season with the salt, pepper, game seasoning and port wine. Stir the eggs and pistachio nuts into the meat mixture.

2 Cut the streaky bacon into slices and line a suitable terrine form with them. Fill the form with the meat mixture, cover with the remaining bacon and cook the terrine in a water bath for about 1¹/₂ hours.

3 Serve the terrine, warm or cold, with Cumberland sauce.

ARDENNES TERRINE

Serves 4–6

1 packet dried morel mushrooms
        (25 g/1 oz)
125 g/4¹/₂ oz onions
3 cloves garlic
1 Tbsp butter
1 bunch mixed herbs
200 g/7 oz shoulder of pork
150 g/5 oz shoulder of veal
175 g/6 oz fat bacon
Salt
1 Tbsp green peppercorns
2 eggs

1 Soak the morels according to packet instructions.

2 Peel the garlic and the onions, cut into cubes and sweat in butter for 5 minutes. Finely chop the herbs.

3 Cut ¹/₃ of the meat into fine cubes. Cut half the bacon into slices. Cut the rest of the meat and the remaining bacon into rough cubes and pass through the mincer.

4 Squeeze out the morels and chop finely. Mix all the ingredients together and then season with salt and pepper.

5 Line a suitable terrine form with the bacon slices and fill the form with the meat mixture. Cover with slices of fat bacon and cook the terrine in a water bath for 1¹/₂ hours.

6 Finally, allow the terrine to cool, weigh down with a heavy object and chill for about 2 days before serving.

ONION TERRINE

Serves 4–6

750 g/1 lb 11 oz onions
4 cloves garlic
3 Tbsp red wine
375 g/13 oz shoulder of pork
375 g/13 oz shoulder of veal
Salt
Pepper
Paprika powder
1 Tbsp chopped herbs
100 g/3½ oz fat bacon
Herbs to garnish

1 Peel the onions and cut into rings. Peel the garlic and finely crush it. Fry the onion and garlic briefly in oil.

2 Deglaze with the red wine and cook for a further 5 minutes.

3 Pass the pork and veal through a mincer on the finest setting.

4 Season the meat with salt, pepper and paprika powder, and mix together with the herbs.

5 Cut the bacon into slices and line a suitable terrine form with it.

6 Place the meat and onions in alternating layers in the form and cover the terrine with slices of bacon

7 Cook the onion terrine in a water bath for 1½ hours. Remove the terrine from the bath, allow to cool, slice, garnish with herbs and serve.

GAME IN ASPIC WITH CRANBERRY AND MUSTARD SAUCE

Serves 6

1 carrot
40 g/1½ oz celeriac
½ a leek
3 hare drumsticks (750 g/1 lb 11 oz)
Salt
Pepper
1 Tbsp oil
2 juniper berries
1 tsp dried thyme
300 ml/10½ fl oz water
4 sheets white gelatine
125 g/4½ oz mushrooms
1 Tbsp port wine
2 Tbsp red wine vinegar
1 Tbsp Madeira
1 Tbsp cranberry sauce
4 tsp hot mustard

1 Trim and wash the vegetables and cut them into small pieces. Rub the hare drumsticks with salt and pepper. Heat the oil in a pan and fry the drumsticks well from all sides.

2 Add the vegetables, juniper berries and thyme. Pour 150 ml/¼ pint of water into the pan, cover and cook for about 30 minutes.

3 Soften the gelatine in a little cold water. Clean the mushrooms and cut into thin slices. Remove the drumsticks from the pan, sieve the stock and bring to the boil. Add the sliced mushrooms and bring to the boil once more. Remove the slices with the skimmer and drain them well.

4 Bone the drumsticks and cut the meat into small slices. Squeeze out the gelatine and dissolve in the lukewarm cooking stock. Add the port wine, vinegar and Madeira and season with salt and pepper.

5 Layer the mushroom and meat slices in a terrine form and cover with the stock. Leave the aspic to stand in the refrigerator overnight to set.

6 Turn the form upside down to free the aspic and cut into slices. To make the sauce, combine the cranberry sauce with the mustard and serve.

WILD BOAR PATÉ

Serves 6

750 g/1¾ lb wild boar meat, in chunks
2 Tbsp oil
4 bay leaves
175 g/6 oz fat bacon
3 onions
Salt
Pepper
50 g/1¾ oz hazelnuts
50 g/1¾ oz pine kernels
125 ml/4½ fl oz cream

1 Brown ⅓ of the meat in hot oil for about 5 minutes together with the crushed juniper berries, then leave to cool. Peel the onions and cut into rough cubes. Also cut the bacon into rough cubes. Pass the remaining meat, the bacon, fried meat chunks and fat from frying through the mincer or blend to a puree in a kitchen mixer. Season the resulting mixture well with salt and pepper.

2 Roughly chop the hazelnuts and, together with the pine kernels, mix well into the meat mixture. Finally, stir in the cream. Fill a paté form with the mixture, cover and bake in a water bath in the oven for 75–90 minutes at 175 °C/355 °F/gas mark 4.

3 Allow the paté to cool and chill in the refrigerator for at least 24 hours before eating. Serve the sliced paté with a spicy cranberry and mustard sauce or with Cumberland sauce.

RILLETES OF WILD BOAR WITH PINK PEPPERCORNS

Serves 6

1.5 kg/3¼ lb neck of wild boar
2 tsp salt
5 Tbsp pink peppercorns
4 onions
2 bay leaves
250 g/9 oz fresh bacon
3 Tbsp gin

1 Salt the meat and put into a large pan with half the peppercorns. Peel the onions, chop roughly into large pieces and, together with the bay leaves, add to the meat. Cut the bacon into very fine cubes and also add to the meat. Pour 3 litres/5¼ pints of water over the ingredients in the pan, bring to the boil and simmer without a lid for 2 to 2½ hours until the meat is tender.

2 Allow the meat to cool somewhat, then remove the meat from the bones and separate the meat fibres with 2 forks. Reduce the cooking liquid to 500 ml/18 fl oz, then carefully stir in the meat, 1 Tbsp peppercorns and the gin.

3 Fill a 1.25 litre/2¼ pint paté form with the mixture, making sure the stock completely covers the meat, and sprinkle with the remaining peppercorns. Cover, and chill in the refrigerator until set.

GOOSE LIVER PATÉ

Serves 4–6

1 large goose liver
Milk
Salt
2–3 truffles
400 g/14 oz filet of pork
60 g/2 oz smoked streaky bacon
6 mushrooms
3 anchovies
The grated peel of 1 untreated lemon
2 eggs
Paté seasoning
Butter
2 thin slices of streaky bacon

1 Soak the goose liver in milk for 2 hours, then dry it and remove the skin. Trim the edges, cut the larger piece in half and sprinkle with salt.

2 Cut the truffles into small pieces. Slice several slits in the liver and insert the truffles. Pass the pork filet, bacon and liver edges through a mincer twice.

3 Sort the mushrooms, brush them clean and cut into small pieces. Finely chop the anchovies. Add them to the minced meat with the lemon peel and mushrooms, and pass this mixture 2 or 3 times through the mincer. Add the eggs, salt and a little paté seasoning.

4 Lightly grease a terrine form with butter and fill it with half the minced meat and mushroom mixture. Lay the liver on this and top with the rest of the mixture. Cover with the thin slices of streaky bacon and close the lid. Fill a deep baking tray with boiling water, place the terrine in it and bake for approximately 2 hours at 100 °C/ 212 °F.

ANCHOVIES IN OIL

Serves 4

400 g/14 oz fresh anchovies
3 lemons
Coarse sea salt
5–6 sprigs parsley
2 cloves garlic
50 g/1¾ oz capers
About 6–8 Tbsp virgin olive oil

1 Wash and dry the anchovies. Remove the heads and spines in one piece. Slit the anchovies open, flatten and carefully remove the remaining fish bones.

2 Lay the fish skin-side down and side by side on a plate. Squeeze the lemons. Sprinkle about ⅔ of the juice over the anchovies and season with salt. Cover and leave to stand in the refrigerator for 8 to 24 hours, basting occasionally with the juice, until the fish becomes white and opaque.

3 Wash and shake dry the parsley, then finely chop. Peel and finely chop the garlic as well.

4 Bring the remaining lemon juice, together with the parsley and the drained capers, to the boil, then leave to cool.

5 Place the anchovies in a suitable container. Stir together the lemon juice mixture and about 4 Tbsp of oil and pour over the anchovies. Finally, top up with sufficient olive oil to cover the anchovies completely. Seal the container airtight and store in the refrigerator until the anchovies are to be eaten.

PICKLED HERRINGS

Serves 4

4 salted herrings weighing
      250 g/9 oz each
125 ml/4¹/₂ fl oz red wine vinegar
75 g/2¹/₂ oz sugar
4 bay leaves
3 Tbsp mustard seeds
5 allspice berries
5 black peppercorns
2 onions (120 g/4¹/₄ oz each)
2 carrots
10 g/¹/₃ oz piece root ginger
50 g/1³/₄ oz piece horseradish

1 Have the herrings filleted by your fishmonger. Soak the fillets in water for 12 hours.

2 Lightly boil the vinegar, 250 ml/9 fl oz of water, the sugar and spices for 10 minutes.

3 Peel the onions, carrots, ginger and horseradish. Cut the onions into thin rings, the carrots into thick slices, the ginger into wafer-thin slices and coarsely grate the horseradish. Rinse the herring fillets, drain and dab dry. Finally, place them, the onion rings, the carrot and ginger slices and the grated horseradish in alternating layers in a jar.

4 Pour the marinade with the spices over the herring fillets. Cover and leave to marinate in the refrigerator for 2 to 3 days.

Tip
The fish becomes firmer when the herring fillets are laid in yoghurt after soaking.

LIGURIAN STYLE
MARINATED SARDINES

Serves 4

750 g/1 lb 11 oz ready to cook sardines
Salt
2 Tbsp flour
3 Tbsp oil
4 red onions
4 cloves garlic
200 ml/7 fl oz red wine vinegar
250 ml/9 fl oz red wine
2 bay leaves
1 tsp sugar
3 Tbsp black olives
2 tsp mustard seeds

1 Rinse and dab dry the sardines, then season with salt and coat with the flour.

2 Heat the oil in a pan and fry the sardines on each side in it for 5 minutes.

3 Peel the onions and cut them into rings. Peel and finely chop the garlic.

4 Combine the onions and garlic, vinegar, wine, bay leaves, sugar, olives and mustard seeds in a pan. Heat through, then leave to stand for about 5 minutes.

5 Pour the cooled liquid over the sardines, cover and allow to stand in the refrigerator for about 2 days before eating.

SEAFOOD IN OIL

Serves 6

500 g/1 lb 2 oz mussels
500 g/1 lb 2 oz Venus mussels or scallops
250 g/ 9 oz squid
200 g/7 oz small calamari
300 g/10 oz prawns
Sea salt
Freshly ground pepper
150 ml/¹/₄ pint olive oil
Juice of 3 lemons

1 Thoroughly scrub the mussels and scallops, removing any barnacles. Remove the beards and thoroughly rinse under flowing water. Discard any damaged and open mussels that do not close when tapped.

2 Clean the squid. Cut open the head and remove the internal organs. Also remove the eyes and hard beak, then rinse and drain. Soften the meat with a meat hammer if necessary.

3 Clean the calamari. Pull the head, tentacles and inner organs from the body. Cut off the heads below the eyes and discard. Put the tentacles to one side. Remove the transparent fish bone from the tubes. Wash and cut the tubes into rings.

4 Wash the prawns. Remove the black digestive cords but leave the tails whole.

5 Bring water to the boil in a large pot. Gently cook the squid in it for about 20 minutes. Add the calamari and prawns, and cook for a further 2 minutes until the prawns turn pink. Remove and drain everything well.

6 Steam the mussels and scallops in a sieve over boiling water for about 2 minutes, until they open (discard any mussels that do not open!). Remove the shells and put the mussels to one side.

7 According to size, cut the squid into pieces and add to the mussels. Also add the calamari and the prawns. Sprinkle everything with sea salt and pepper. Beat together the oil and the lemon juice, pour over the seafood, cover and leave to stand in the refrigerator for at least 12 to 24 hours.

8 Season the seafood before serving and garnish with parsley and lemon.

RECIPE INDEX

Picture Credits
The publisher is grateful to the following firms, agencies and organisations for their friendly permission to use photographs and recipes:
CMA, pp. 13, 15, 26, 31, 34, 35, 99, 103; Fuchs Gewürze, p. 135; Galbani, p. 87; Kölner Zucker, p. 105;
Sopexa, p. 86; Supress, pp. 59, 89, 92, 95; Verband der deutschen Fruchtsaft-Industrie e.V., p. 30
All other photos: Naumann & Göbel Verlagsgesellschaft mbH, Cologne